DISASTER MANAGEMENT IN BRITISH LIBRARIES

PROJECT REPORT
WITH
GUIDELINES FOR LIBRARY MANAGERS

Graham Matthews and Paul Eden

Library and Information Research Report 109

The opinions expressed in this report are those of the authors and not necessarily of the British Library. The British Library and the authors cannot be held responsible for any damage from the use of the guidelines in this report.

ISBN 0 7123 3306 1

Printed and bound in Great Britain by
Biddles Ltd, Guildford and King's Lynn

Abstract

Disaster management in British libraries, a research project funded by the British Library Research and Development Department, was undertaken between March 1995-April 1996 by Graham Matthews, Lecturer and Project Head and Paul Eden, Research Associate, in the Department of Information and Library Studies, Loughborough University, England.

The project aimed to achieve an overview of current disaster management practice in British libraries and to produce guidelines on disaster management based on good practice for library and information service managers. This was achieved through analysis of written disaster control plans; review of the literature, including existing advice and guidance; consultation with project Advisory Group members; interviews with not only librarians but others in different areas with expertise in, and experience of, disaster management. 53 people from 34 different organisations were visited and interviewed, including archivists, fire officers, museums officers, an architect, and representatives from commercial binders, disaster salvage and recovery companies, heritage organisations, an insurance company and loss adjusters.

The findings are presented as *Disaster management in British libraries: project report with guidelines for library managers*. The report provides background for the practical guidelines and highlights and discusses key issues such as advice, expertise and services, business and service continuity, communication, fire detection and suppression systems, responsibility for disaster management, risk assessment and the written disaster control plan. The guidelines are presented under four main headings, widely recognised as four key stages of disaster management: Prevention, Preparedness, Reaction and Recovery. These are further divided into main areas of activity within each of these such as Buildings, contents and facilities, Collections, Computers, Emergency equipment and supplies, Human resources, Insurance and Security. Major actions are highlighted in boxes, with specific advice and information alongside as 'bullet points'. Recommendations aimed at librarians concerned with the day to day practice of disaster management are incorporated throughout the guidelines. Recommendations aimed at a broader professional audience are included at the end of the report. These address issues such as awareness raising, disaster management advice, expertise and services, risk assessment, training and further research into areas such as conservation and salvage treatments, including associated costs, and health and safety. The guidelines also include a select bibliography.

The authors

Graham Matthews is a Lecturer in the Department of Information and Library Studies, Loughborough University. He has been a lecturer for ten years. Prior to this he worked in public and academic libraries. His main research interest is preservation management, a subject which he also teaches in the Department. From 1987-1995, he was a member of the British Library National Preservation Advisory Committee Education Panel. He has had a keen interest in disaster management, a major aspect of preservation in libraries, since the late 1980s and has written and presented various papers on the subject. Previous research includes: *Preservation of Russian and Soviet materials in British libraries*, Liverpool Polytechnic Press, 1991. (British Library Research and Development report 6033); *Preservation policies and practice in British libraries: a ten-year review, 1983-1992*, with Professor John Feather and Paul Eden, funded by The Leverhulme Trust. He is co-author with these two colleagues of *Preservation management: policies and practices in British libraries*. (Gower, 1996).

Paul Eden is a Research Associate in the Department of Information and Library Studies, Loughborough University, where he has worked since 1992, He has co-authored several papers on preservation issues, including disaster management, for the professional literature, and a recently published book on preservation policies and practices.

DISASTER MANAGEMENT IN BRITISH LIBRARIES
PROJECT REPORT
WITH
GUIDELINES FOR LIBRARY MANAGERS

Contents

Appendices

PART TWO. DISASTER MANAGEMENT: GUIDELINES FOR LIBRARY MANAGERS

Acknowledgements

The support of the British Library Research and Development Department, which funded this research, is gratefully acknowledged.

We are grateful for the support and advice of the project Advisory Group members, Professor John Feather, Dean, School of Education and Humanities, Loughborough University, Valerie Ferris, (then) National Preservation Officer, National Preservation Office based at the British Library, Dr Helen Forde, Head of Preservation, Public Record Office, Hilary Hammond, County Librarian, Norfolk County Library and Information Service, Chris Hunt, Director and University Librarian, The John Rylands University of Manchester Library, Stephanie Kenna, Research Analyst, British Library Research and Development Department, John McIntyre, Director of Preservation, National Library of Scotland, Margaret Saunders, Group Librarian, Commercial Union Asset Management Ltd.

We are also grateful to those libraries and archives which sent us copies of their disaster control plans (see Appendix B), and to all those whom we visited and interviewed, or who otherwise provided us with information (see Appendix C).

Whilst we are grateful to all those individuals and organisations who so willingly gave us so much of their time, any inaccuracies and omissions in the text are ours.

Part one
Project Report

1. Introduction

The concept of disaster management is not new in British libraries. The mid to late 1980s, in particular, was a period of awareness raising and activity: the well-known and widely-praised National Library of Scotland's *Planning manual for disaster control in Scottish libraries and record offices* was published in 1985 (Anderson and McIntyre, 1985); the British Library published an outline disaster control plan in 1987 (Tregarthen Jenkin, 1987); the National Preservation Office (NPO), based at the British Library, co-sponsored a competition on the subject in 1988, publishing the winning plan and two others the following year (NPO/Riley Dunn and Wilson, 1989); and, in 1988, the NPO produced a video, *If disaster strikes!* (NPO, 1988). Two major disasters abroad, at the Los Angeles Central Public Library in 1986 (Butler, 1986) and the Academy of Sciences Library, Leningrad in 1988 (Matthews, 1988), and their aftermath, received broad coverage in the professional literature and were thus made well-known to British librarians. The IRA bomb in the City of London in 1992 and its effect on the Commercial Union Library, in particular, served as further warning (Saunders, 1993).

By the early 1990s, however, many British libraries still did not have disaster control plans - a key indicator that disaster management is being formally addressed (Eden, Feather and Matthews, 1994). It would appear that the attitude 'it won't happen here' prevailed in many libraries. Such complacency or low priority afforded to disaster management was to be shaken by the fire which destroyed Norwich Central Library at the beginning of August 1994 (Fire rekindles debate, 1994). The flood at the Fawcett Library, London Guildhall University, later that month, had further professional impact (Wise, 1995). Library managers realised that it *could* happen to them, and that they needed to find out how to address disaster management in their own libraries and organisations.

This British Library Research and Development Department funded research project aims to meet the need for up-to-date, practical information and guidance. It highlights current good practice in libraries and related fields. It provides a broad base of information drawn from the practical experience and expertise of not only librarians, but others such as archivists, fire officers, insurers, loss adjusters, museums officers, commercial binders, disaster salvage and recovery companies and heritage organisations. This is supplemented by analysis of written disaster control plans and a survey of the literature. The project's findings are presented in two parts: *Part One. Project Report* and *Part Two. Disaster management: guidelines for library managers.*

Our key findings are incorporated in the Guidelines. The Report underlines and discusses the broader main issues brought to our attention by interviewees and respondents and indicates some areas which we feel require further consideration or investigation. It also includes comments from interviewees which enrich and enliven the discussion. Unless available in the public domain all comments are unattributable, thus respecting the confidentiality of those we interviewed or who sent us information.

The Report and Guidelines are aimed at library and information managers working in the wide range of libraries and information services in Britain today. For the sake of brevity, they are referred to collectively as 'librarian' and 'library' throughout the Report and Guidelines. The research's focus has been on the British situation, with an emphasis on British experience and documentation. (This is not to ignore the large and helpful literature on disaster management from North America and elsewhere, examples of which are included in the Bibliography.)

It should be stressed that the Guidelines are not intended for use as a disaster reaction document. Rather, they should be used as a starting point for those addressing disaster management for the first time or who are reviewing existing procedures.

Individual organisations must decide for themselves their own disaster management needs, based on a consideration of their own resources and other priorities. In addition, each library must formulate its own written disaster control plan. Whilst those devising disaster control plans need to consult guidelines, talk to colleagues with relevant experience, look at other libraries' plans and read the literature, each plan needs to be building specific and to work within a unique organisational context. We, therefore do not prescribe minimum requirements but offer a broad picture and trust that this will be of use to managers in different libraries and information services.

No matter how many guidelines are consulted or precautions taken, the incidence of disasters in libraries can never be totally removed. Good disaster management, however, can both help to prevent disasters occurring or minimise their effect. We hope that this report and guidelines will be of assistance in the disaster management process in your library or information service.

1.1 Terminology

The terms disaster, disaster control plan and disaster management as used throughout the Report and Guidelines are described below.

A precise definition of *disaster* is not straightforward; it is easy to think of exceptions and the term is often used emotively. For the purposes of this research, the following simple, working definition of disaster as applied to library and information services is used: a disaster is "any incident which threatens human safety and/or damages, or threatens to damage, a library's buildings, collections, contents, facilities or services".

Thus, libraries are vulnerable to a variety of disasters, man-made or natural, including fire (for example, caused by electrical faults or arson) or flood (for example, caused by burst pipes or heavy rain). The scale of a disaster may also vary considerably, ranging from a few bays of water-damaged books to total destruction of a library and its contents. In addition, inadequate maintenance and security of buildings, poor housekeeping or inappropriate storage and environmental conditions may increase the risk and impact of such occurrences.

A *disaster control plan* is a clear, concise document which outlines preventive and preparatory measures intended to reduce potential risks, and which also provides details of reaction and recovery procedures to be undertaken in the event of a disaster to minimise its effect. (Examples of published disaster control plans are included in the Bibliography.)

Disaster management includes much more than the formulation of a written disaster control plan. It encompasses broader management issues such as finance, risk assessment and training. Using the term disaster management also emphasises that it ought to be treated as a key area of library management and afforded due attention by senior management within the library and any parent organisation.

Graham Matthews and Paul Eden

Department of Information and Library Studies

Loughborough University

April 1996

4

2. Aims and objectives

The research set out to:

- identify the range and scope of current activities and expertise relevant to effective disaster management in British libraries and information services

- achieve an overview of disaster management activity to date and likely future developments in British libraries, archives and other relevant agencies

- achieve an overview of the written disaster control plans currently used by libraries and determine criteria for their effective assessment and implementation

- identify and investigate any national, regional, local and inter-organisational cooperative disaster management activities and initiatives

- investigate disaster management policy and activity abroad

- produce guidelines on disaster management for library managers based on good practice.

3. Methodology and summary of responses

The research was undertaken between March 1995-April 1996 and was based on six main elements:

- acquisition and analysis of written disaster control plans
- literature survey
- interviews and visits
- requests for information
- project Advisory Group
- attendance at conferences, seminars and meetings

The following describes the methodology relating to each of these elements.

3.1 Acquisition and analysis of written disaster control plans

Disaster management in British libraries builds on an earlier project, *Preservation policies and practices in British libraries, a ten year review, 1983-1992,* which the project team carried out with Professor John Feather at the Department of Information and Library Studies, Loughborough University in 1993 (Feather, Matthews and Eden, 1996). As its title suggests this earlier project looked at a whole range of preservation issues including disaster management.

In April 1995 the project team wrote to all of the 486 identifiable libraries (177 academic, 132 public and 177 national and special) which responded to the 1993 survey asking them for a copy of any written disaster control plans they might have. Any plans received were analysed using a checklist of criteria built up from existing guidelines and published plans, not to evaluate or criticise individual plans, but to:

- identify the range and scope of current activities and expertise as demonstrated by those practising in the field
- achieve an insight into current disaster management practice
- determine criteria for the effective assessment of disaster control plans generally.

Appendix A contains a copy of one of the letters sent to the libraries which replied to the 1993 survey asking them for a copy of their written disaster control plans. This was the letter sent to libraries replying to the earlier survey saying that they had a disaster control plan (written or otherwise). A similar letter, suitably amended, was sent to the libraries which replied saying that they did not have such a plan.

3.1.1 responses

Replies were received from 388 libraries (79.84%), including 150 academic (an 84.75% response), 113 public (an 85.61% response) and 125 national and special (a 70.62% response). 78 libraries (20.10%) said that they had a written disaster control plan; 36 academic (24.00%), 17 public (15.04%) and 25 national and special (20.00%). Copies of plans were received from 62 of these 78 libraries. A further copy was obtained from a special library not included in the earlier survey, making 63 plans received in all. Appendix B contains a list of libraries which sent a copy of their disaster control plans.

The plans received varied greatly in size, ranging from a single sheet of A4 paper to a full A4 ring binder. This, not surprisingly, was largely a reflection of the size of the library and the number of staff available. The single page 'Contingency Plan' received from a small independent special library, for example, is effectively a 16 point checklist to remind the librarian who to contact and giving instructions such as "Cancel newspaper and periodicals where possible".

Although several plans were in the form of a continuous document (albeit with separate headings and subheadings), many more were organised into separate sections such as Disaster Prevention, Disaster Control Team, Disaster Control Materials/equipment and Salvage Priorities. One archive divided part of its plan into the different tasks staff might need to carry out in the event of a disaster (for example, sorting damaged materials, drying damaged materials and removing damaged or threatened items) and used different coloured paper for each of these sections. Analysis of these plans forms the basis for the *Written disaster control plan* sections in the guidelines in part two.

3.2 Literature survey

A comprehensive literature survey was undertaken. Some of the most helpful and interesting items found during this survey are contained in the Bibliography at the end of the guidelines in part two. Many of these items themselves include bibliographies and references to other useful sources.

Libraries visited included the British Library Information Science Service (BLISS), the Fire Protection

Association library and the Heath and Safety Exectutive Information Services' library at Sheffield.

3.3 Interviews and visits

A series of interviews with people in organisations within and outside the library profession was carried out to look at the practical aspects of implementing written disaster control plans within a broader disaster management perspective. Those visited included:

- librarians
- archivists
- museums services
- heritage organisations
- disaster salvage and recovery companies
- commercial binders
- fire officers
- loss adjusters
- an insurance company heavily involved in local authority insurance
- an architect experienced in library design.

Interviewees in libraries, archives and museums services were selected because they were responsible for disaster management within their own organisations or because they had experienced various types of disaster. Particular insurers, commercial binders and disaster salvage or restoration companies were selected because they were the organisations most often cited as external sources of advice and expertise in the written disaster control plans which were sent to the project team. Interviews were conducted using a semi-structured interview schedule, an example of which is contained in Appendix C. In all, 53 people from 34 different organisations were interviewed. Appendix D contains a list of the interviewees and organisations visited.

3.4 Requests for information

The project team wrote to 80 professional bodies, trade associations and commercial organisations active in the field of disaster management in the United Kingdom and abroad requesting information on "disaster management policies and practice, including details of any free or priced publications and courses". Those approached included business continuity consultancies, computer recovery companies, heritage organisations and professional bodies representing archives, libraries and museums. Selection was based on suggestions from Advisory Group members, interviewees, professional contacts known to the Project Head and information in recently published literature. Appendix E contains a list of organisations contacted.

3.5 Project Advisory Group

An Advisory Group met three times during the course of the research bringing to the research valuable and wide-ranging disaster management expertise, experience and practical knowledge gained from a variety of different backgrounds and activities. More specifically the Advisory Group:

- suggested contacts and sources of specialist information
- suggested organisations and individuals for interviews and visits
- commented on and augmented the criteria for assessment of written disaster control plans
- made suggestions and recommendations throughout the course of the research
- read through and advised on the final draft guidelines on disaster management for library managers.

Appendix F contains a list of Advisory Group members.

3.6 Attendance at conferences, seminars and meetings

The project team visited a number of conferences, seminars and meetings during the course of the research, both as delegates and as speakers. This afforded opportunities for disseminating preliminary findings and obtaining valuable feedback. Appendix G contains a list of conferences, seminars and meetings attended by the project team members.

4. Discussion of main findings

The main research findings are presented and discussed under five broad headings:

- responsibility for disaster management

- prevention

- preparedness

- reaction

- recovery

These headings represent core areas of disaster management activity as understood and described by interviewees. More specific issues are discussed under each of these headings. They are also incorporated in the guidelines.

4.1 Responsibility for disaster management

It is important that disaster management is afforded proper attention by senior management and that the necessary staffing and resourcing structures are put in place. These will inevitably vary according to each library's particular circumstances. The following, however, looks at the main areas of responsibility and actions which should be covered.

Effective disaster management requires, as one fire safety adviser put it, "Management, management and more management". Comments from interviewees and analysis of disaster control plans suggest three clear areas of managerial responsibility. These areas are discussed below under three descriptive 'job titles': Disaster Manager, Disaster Reaction Manager and Disaster Recovery Manager. This is done not to suggest that the disaster management responsibilities should necessarily be separated in this way, but to make discussion of these areas of responsibility easier. Libraries may decide that a particular member of staff should assume all three roles; indeed, the size and staffing levels of the library may well dictate this. In addition, libraries will need to be aware of and comply with any relevant organisational policies such as those relating to reporting procedures, line management responsibilities and security matters (for example, liaison with the emergency services).

Libraries should also bear in mind that, as one interviewee put it, "Even senior managers go on holiday, or are off sick". Those responsible for disaster management must, therefore, ensure that at least one other member of staff is able to deputise for them in their absence. Just as importantly, they must ensure that their deputies receive the same training as themselves.

4.1.1 Disaster Manager

The Disaster Manager, who must be a senior member of staff, need not be responsible for day to day disaster management which, as we will see, depends upon the vigilance and cooperation of all staff, and which can be better overseen by line managers and others with specific responsibilities such as Health and Safety Officers. Rather, the Disaster Manager's role will be to ensure that disaster management is supported at the highest level within the library's parent organisation, that sufficient resources are made available to finance it and that any problems and requirements are brought to the attention of other senior managers. In order to do so, as one commercial librarian with disaster experience pointed out, "It may be necessary...[for the Disaster Manager]...to take the initiative rather than wait for others to involve you as the library may well be near the

11

bottom of organisational priorities".

The Disaster Manager must also be able to build up a rapport with staff in other departments within the parent organisation, as the research findings suggest that it may often prove difficult for the library to obtain the information which it requires from them for effective disaster managment. In one library visited, for example, the librarian responsible for disaster management "spent a considerable amount of time" trying to ascertain whether or not there was an organisational plan already in existence, and if so who was responsible for it. She also found it very difficult to find out if and when the library's electrical wiring had been checked, and only received "assurances" that fire safety equipment and alarms had been tested properly. Other librarians interviewed highlighted similar experiences.

As we will see throughout the report and the guidelines the library will often need to seek advice from other departments such as estates, finance and security. It is, therefore, extremely important that an atmosphere of mutual trust and cooperation is established. The Disaster Manager's role is thus crucial.

4.1.2 Disaster Reaction Manager

The Disaster Reaction Manager, as the name suggests, is the person with responsibility for coordinating all aspects of an immediate disaster response. Interviewees stressed the need for the Disaster Reaction Manager to be a senior member of staff with the authority to make spending decisions, but emphasised above all the personal qualities which he or she should possess. The disaster recovery expert who said that libraries "have to select the best person for the job rather than the most senior..[as]...it will be beyond the capabilities of even some highly experienced managerial staff to cope in such extremely stressful situations as might be faced" was typical in this respect.

The Disaster Reaction Manager must have the ability, in the words of the same disaster recovery expert, to make decisions "quickly, and often several at the same time". To do so, he or she must be able to take advice from other staff with particular expertise and experience, and, as one librarian with disaster experience said "allow expert staff to make decisions and stand by these decisions afterwards". These views were emphasised still further by another disaster recovery expert who said the worst and most expensive cause of damage following a disaster is "poor management - the patients are dying, but nobody can make a decision".

12

In addition, the Disaster Reaction Manager will need to be calm and level-headed, have good communication skills, be a good organiser and be able to coordinate a response which might involve the emergency services, several sections and departments within the parent organisation and external organisations such as salvage and restoration companies. The Disaster Reaction Manager must also have a good knowledge of the library building, its contents and its facilities. It is significant, for example, that the fire officers interviewed said that they prefer to deal with a single person who has this knowledge when called to an incident.

4.1.3 Disaster Recovery Manager

Following a more serious disaster the library may need to appoint a Disaster Recovery Manager to take responsibility for various aspects of short, medium and long term recovery too complex to be undertaken without some form of centralised control. The Disaster Recovery Manager may need, for example, to find temporary accommodation to house staff and ensure service and/or business continuity and access (including access to networked computer and other electronic computer-based systems), arrange for the safe temporary storage of undamaged stock or oversee the successful completion of any conservation work which needs to be carried out. This will involve close liaison with the Disaster Reaction Manager, at least during the intitial stages of recovery.

Financial considerations will be crucial, and according to a disaster recovery expert "in any significant disaster situation there should be one person in charge, with mechanisms in place for allocating money and other resources quickly and efficiently". This view was supported by another disaster recovery expert who said, "There may be no time for the usual tendering procedures, and money will be spent surprisingly quickly".

4.2 Prevention

Prevention is better than cure! Prevention focuses on the identification of risks to people, collections, buildings, contents and facilities, and the subsequent actions needed to reduce these risks, thereby lessening the likelihood of a disaster occurring. It is a key and vital step in disaster management.

This section will consider:

- risk assessment
- inspections and maintenance of buildings, contents and facilities
- staff awareness and vigilance
- valuable items and collections
- smoke detectors and sprinklers
- computers

4.2.1 Risk assessment

All the disaster recovery experts interviewed stressed the fact that disasters - other than natural catastrophes - are seldom caused by a single incident. Rather, in the words of one such expert, "they tend to be the result of a number of relatively minor events or situations occurring either together or, more usually, over a period of time". Assessments of the risks to people, buildings, collections, contents and facilities is accordingly the first and most important step in disaster prevention, and a necessary prerequisite to writing a disaster control plan.

Risk assessment if properly carried out, however, involves several different areas of expertise, many, if not most, of which lie outside the librarian's normal work experience. Fire, flood and security risks, for example, will all need to be assessed. Consequently, librarians responsible for disaster management will almost inevitably have to take expert advice from others. One of the first tasks they must do, therefore, is identify the areas for which they require more information, and having identified them, seek advice.

In addition, comments from one buildings and facilities manager suggested that some libraries may need to take a more holistic approach to risk management. Within her own library, for example, 'disaster control planning' used to mean 'collections' rather than 'buildings', but as she pointed out, threats to buildings are very often threats to collections; "protecting the one can protect the other".

Having identified any risks the library will then need to try to remove or reduce them. In many cases this will be a relatively simple matter. For example, clearing cardboard boxes, waste paper or other refuse from basement areas to remove a fire hazard. In some cases, however, building and repair work may be necessary. Libraries may then need to draw up a costed and prioritised work programme based on the likelihood of a particular risk leading to a disaster and the likely implications for the library should that disaster occur (for example, how it might affect core services or damage special collections).

4.2.1.1 advice on risk assessments

In larger organisations much expertise is likely to be available in-house. In the first instance, therefore, (where available) libraries should ask buildings, estates, insurance and computing services personnel for advice. Even if these departments are unable to help the library themselves they may well be able to suggest suitable external sources of advice.

Libraries may also have their own archivists or conservators who can help with collection risks assessments. Alternatively, many interviewees found that archivists and conservators in other organisations were often more than willing to offer advice and help.

Risk assessments carried out by external consultants can be particularly advantageous as, in addition to highlighting any problems which need to be addressed, they may help to raise the profile of the library and its needs with the parent organisation. One academic library, for example, had a fire risk assessment carried out by the Fire Protection Association. The librarian said that she found its report extremely useful as it both "highlighted what the library should be doing" and helped to "concentrate the need for action in the minds of Buildings and Estates personnel".

Libraries should not, however, overlook the free advice available from their local emergency services. Fire authorities were invariably singled out by those interviewees who had been in contact with them as being especially helpful. Fire authorities are required by the 1947 Fire Services Act to visit premises to give advice "when requested...in respect of buildings and other property in the area of the fire authority as to fire prevention, restricting the spread of fires, and means of escape in case of fire" (Section 1(i)(f)). Similarly, local Crime Prevention Officers were recommended by several interviewees as useful sources of advice on security issues such as fitting locks to doors and windows.

Whoever the library looks to for advice it is important, as one disaster recovery expert put it, to "know their language". Experts often seem to be using 'a foreign language' confusing to the layperson. They may even give advice which conflicts with that of other experts.

Experts are also used to being asked for particular pieces of advice which may lead them to make not unreasonable assumptions. Do not presume, for example, that just because the local fire authority's Fire Safety Officer has visited the library and advised on fire safety that the library's collections will be 'safe'. According to a senior fire officer, Fire Safety Officers are usually only approached for advice on what needs to be done in order to comply with fire safety and building legislation, and will probably presume that this is what the library wants. Unfortunately for the library's collections, this legislation is concerned only with human safety and not with protecting buildings and their contents *per se*.

Libraries should, therefore, always be very specific when asking for risk assessments to be carried out, and this will be particularly important if a third party such as a Health and Safety Officer is involved. In the case of collections, for example, whoever is carrying out the risk assessment must know exactly which individual items or collections need to be protected and to what degree. Furthermore, interviewees, inside and outside the library profession, stressed that when commissioning risk assessments libraries should only approach reputable individuals and organisations such as those well-known within their own professions with proven track records.

4.2.2 Inspections and maintenance of buildings, contents and facilities

In addition to carrying out risk assessments, libraries should ensure that their buildings, contents and facilities are regularly inspected and maintained. This will enable 'minor' problems to be identified and rectified before they become more serious and either cause a disaster themselves or lead to even greater damage should one occur for any other reason. One librarian, for example, described how, during building tours carried out to produce floor plans, several libraries in her local authority discovered that taps on stopcocks - essential to turn off the water supply in an emergency - were seized tight.

Inspections must be recorded along with any problems discovered and there must be clear written procedures to ensure that all necessary work is carried out. Several interviewees believed that one of the most effective ways of supporting this process on a daily basis was to have a defect book. In fact, the Pearson Report (*An*

Inquiry into the Fire at the Norwich Central Library) recommends that the Central Library keep a defect book, suggesting that it should be "inspected monthly by the Principal Librarian who should indicate that the defects have been brought to his attention" and adding that "the Property Inspector responsible for the building should also examine the defects book on a regular basis" (Pearson, 1995, p. 61).

It is also essential to ensure that any building work carried out meets required standards. For example, as one senior fire officer pointed out it is no good having the right fire-resistant blocks in ceiling spaces above fire-doors to prevent the spread of fire if they are not fitted flush with the doors below, as this will allow fire to get into the ceiling space via the gaps.

4.2.3 Staff awareness and vigilance

While regular inspections of buildings and contents and clearly laid-out reporting procedures are essential, the goodwill and cooperation of staff is just as important. As several interviewees pointed out, for example, the effectiveness of a defect book depends not only on staff being aware of its existence, but also on them being 'risk and safety conscious' enough to notice problems and take the trouble to report them.

All staff must be encouraged to be vigilant regarding the everyday safety and security of themselves and colleagues, users, collections, buildings, contents and facilities. They must be aware of reporting procedures and who is responsible for seeing that any reported problems are dealt with. They must know what steps they can take to reduce the likelihood of a disaster occurring. All these will be important aspects of the library's disaster management training programmes. Good housekeeing is essential.

In return, library managers have a duty to ensure that any reported problems are properly dealt with. If not, then they should not be surprised if staff simply stop reporting them.

Many of the risk and safety issues which staff will need to know about are, of course, covered by health and safety legislation and libraries will in any case need to ensure that they comply with minimum requirements. Suggestions for further reading on health and safety issues are included in the Bibliography at the end of the guidelines in part two.

4.2.4 Valuable items and collections

Although disaster management is concerned with minimising the risks to all the library's collections, most libraries will nevertheless have some items or collections which they will wish to afford greater protection. Such protection will usually include optimising environmental conditions and/or taking enhanced security precautions in a particular area of the library. Several interviewees with disaster experience, however, pointed out that libraries also need to consider the question of how easily these items or collections could be removed from the building if threatened by a disaster. In one special library visited, for example, an important collection of flags and banners which had previously been threatened during a disaster was moved to the library's administration office next to the main entrance so that staff could get them out quickly should the need arise (security precautions having been taken). Unfortunately, as well as having limited resources, libraries are public buildings, and the answer to the question "Why do librarians always put their most valuable items and archives in the basement" (a typical comment from interviewees outside the library profession) is often that there is simply no other place to keep them.

Mistakes, however, may be made even when precautions have been taken with the best of intentions. Several interviewees with disaster experience stressed the importance of always thinking through all the things that could go wrong. One interviewee, for example, described how he was once taken round a county library where he was proudly shown a brand new environmentally-controlled special collections room; unfortunately pushing aside the suspended ceiling above the collections revealed a network of water pipes.

4.2.5 Smoke detectors and sprinklers

The librarians interviewed were uncertain regarding the benefits or otherwise of installing smoke detectors and sprinkler systems. In particular, they found literature on sprinklers very confusing. For example, those responsible for disaster management in one library which had suffered a disaster had considered installing a sprinkler system during refurbishment, but found the literature "divided" on the subject.

On the other hand, the consensus of opinion among the insurers, loss adjusters and salvage experts interviewed was that libraries should install smoke detectors rather than heat detectors, and that sprinklers offer the best protection against fire. Sprinklers are designed to operate only in areas directly affected by fire and can, therefore, contain a fire at source before it is able to spread, a significant threat in open-plan buildings such as the majority of libraries. These experts also suggested that, whereas, badly fire-damaged materials must be discarded, water-damaged books and other materials can usually be successfully salvaged and restored to an acceptable condition. Indeed, as several of them pointed out any fire fighters called to the scene are likely to discharge far more water than the sprinklers.

The same experts were also keen to point out that modern sprinkler systems are far more reliable than in the past. This view is supported by "Independent statistics [which] show that the chance of discharge resulting from a manufacturing defect is 1 in 14 million, and from all causes, 1 in half a million per year of service" (Brown, 1994, p. 7) (the latter figure includes factors unlikely to be a problem for libraries such as damage by forklift trucks), and records showing that "on average there is only one sprinkler head failure per 1,000,000 heads installed per year" (Municipal Mutual, 1991, section 3.1).

For protecting particularly valuable items or collections, one disaster expert suggested that libraries may wish to consider the so-called 'Intelligent Sprinklers' developed in the USA. Installed by, among others, the Library of Congress. Intelligent Sprinklers enable fires to be "detected and controlled at the earliest opportunity and only the minimum amount of water necessary to control the fire is discharged" (Stimpson, 1994, p. 10).

The Pearson Report supports these views and it is worth quoting the relevant passage at some length:

> "There is a long time, indeed almost traditional, antipathy on the part of Librarians towards sprinkler systems. This is perfectly understandable because they fear the water damage to their stocks of books which could result from the sprinkler heads discharging accidentally or as a result of a false alarm, and a perception that in such an event the whole sprinkler system will begin a discharge giving rise to enormous damage. These fears are in my view wrong ... In fully sprinklered premises automatic sprinklers can be expected to control fires in over 95% of cases and, significantly, in over 90% of cases the fire will be controlled within the system's design area of operation. Modern systems have become extremely sophisticated and the risk of accidental discharge is now so low that it can be almost entirely discounted" (Pearson, 1995, p. 45).

Pearson also suggests that "Where fears remain consideration can be given to the installation of a mist system, the accidental activation of which gives rise to very little damage to books or other documents" (Pearson, 1995, p. 45).

Nevertheless, libraries must be realistic. As one senior fire officer commented, in the vast majority of cases creating a 'totally safe' library would probably be "both prohibitively expensive and impractical given the fact that libraries need to be open and welcoming to their users". Libraries can only do what is reasonable given their resources and overall missions.

4.2.6 Computers

Although interviewees were invariably aware that computer systems, software and files must always be backed-up, and that wherever possible copies of software and files should be kept off-site, they were equally aware that this is something which is a lot easier said than done. Typical of comments were those of one senior librarian who said that although dealing with networked computer systems was "fairly straightforward" (but see below), it was "a lot more difficult to keep control of software and files held on PCs", and that although individuals may be actively encouraged to keep backup disks "it is very hard to know whether or not they are doing so". Several interviewees, therefore, thought it was essential to have a clear policy on backing-up data on PCs which was known to, and understood by, all staff, with regular checks and software audits carried out to ensure that policy is followed.

Theft was also highlighted as a particular problem regarding computer hardware, with thieves targeting monitors, central processing units, keyboards and, more recently, computer chips. Interviewees suggested that in addition to highlighting the need for security and staff vigilance, theft once again underlined the need to keep backup copies of software and files kept on hard disks.

4.2.6.1 liaison with service providers

As several interviewees pointed out, libraries probably have to rely more on others for the effective protection of their networked computer systems than for any other area of disaster management. Computer departments within the parent organisation and/or external service providers are likely to be responsible for backing-up system software and files, the day to day running of automated library systems and providing emergency facilities and disaster recovery responses to cope with system hard-disk crashes, BT network failures and power outages. In one public library service visited, for example, the library's own support services are responsible for application software and end-user problems, while the county's IT Services department are responsible for all maintenance and system backups.

Libraries should, therefore, ensure that they are fully aware of existing precautions taken by computer departments and/or external service providers, including system security, recovery, temporary service and access arrangements. Once these are known they should decide whether or not they are adequate, and if not discuss ways in which they can be improved. If current practice does not include a service level agreement or contract one or other should be considered.

4.3 Preparedness

Being prepared should enable the library to respond more quickly and more effectively to disasters, thereby reducing their effects and facilitating recovery.

This section will consider:

- written disaster control plans
- training
- advice, expertise and services
- emergency equipment and supplies
- insurance
- service continuity and access

4.3.1 Written disaster control plans

Although there may be differences of opinion between interviewees regarding some aspects of disaster management, there was general agreement between all those interviewed that each library should prepare a written disaster control plan. Having a written plan means that staff have written instructions on how to raise the alarm, who to contact and what it is they should be doing as soon as a disaster occurs or is discovered. This is extremely important. As one fire officer said "It is surprising how many people...[often used to having managerial responsibility]...simply cannot comprehend what is happening around them during an emergency situation". A set of clear, simple instructions to get staff started can help them to get over any initial shock and ensure that they do not have time to worry about the situation. Staff also need to know in advance what they can do to mitigate the effects of a disaster on people, collections, buildings, contents and facilities and where they can obtain any necessary advice, expertise and services.

All interviewees with disaster experience, however, stressed the fact that disaster reaction and recovery needs to be flexible. Accordingly, a good written disaster control plan "will rarely prescribe a single response because the shape and nature of disasters are unpredictable. It is more likely to contain a compendium of information, options and procedures from which the recovery team can choose the most appropriate course of action having assessed the actual situation on the ground" (Hyams, 1993, p. 7).

As well as being flexible written plans should not be overloaded with too much detail. One interviewee,

22

very experienced in large-scale disaster management both in libraries and other organisations, emphasised the importance of this, saying that when writing the disaster control plan the aim should "not be to create a document containing everything that needs to be done following a disaster". For example, a librarian in a national library with considerable disaster management experience said that plans need not contain a lot of information on how to handle every type of library material however badly damaged. Rather, instructions should concentrate on "damage limitation" with a clear understanding that, where doubts exist, "expert advice should be sought as soon as possible".

The need for flexibility and simplicity was echoed by interviewees from outside the library profession such as salvage experts, fire officers and conservators, who advocated having a separate or 'pull-out' section with simple easy to follow instructions for immediate use during the reaction stage. These same interviewees also underlined the need to include guidance which will help others called to the scene to react more quickly and effectively. Within this context floor plans showing individual items and collections prioritised for salvage and the whereabouts of stopcocks, power points, isolation valves and fuse boxes were considered to be especially important. So were flowcharts outlining in a 'step-by-step' format actions such as raising the alarm and handling and salvaging damaged materials for drying and other treatments.

Written plans, therefore, should be seen, in the words of one librarian as "blueprints for action" which give guidance on the actions and measures which may need to be taken immediately following a disaster (or at least as soon as it is discovered) and later during the reaction and recovery stages, both by library staff and others, such as the emergency services or salvage and restoration experts, who may be called to the scene. The written disaster control plan thus acts as a focal point for disaster management, and is a basic requirement for quick and effective disaster reaction and recovery. It is a first and most important step in disaster preparedness. It is important, however, to remember that no written disaster control plan is ever truly 'finished'. The plan should be reviewed at least annually, and will need to be updated following any staff changes which affect the plan such as the departure of a named contact, changes in accommodation and refurbishment. It must also be supported by a comprehensive programme of training.

Further details of what should be included in the written disaster control plan and its physical format are contained in the guidelines in part two in the section on Preparedness.

4.3.1.1 responsibility for writing the disaster control plan

For most interviewees the question of who should be given responsibility for writing the disaster control plan and how best to proceed depends on various practical considerations within the library itself, and structural factors within the organisation as a whole. Practical considerations within the library include individual workloads, staff numbers and available expertise, while structural factors include the size of the parent organisation, its prevailing ethos and relationships between its different departments and sections.

In a small special library, for example, it is likely that only one person will have responsibility for writing the plan; indeed the librarian may be the only professional member of staff. A large academic library, on the other hand, might need to adopt a 'committee' approach, giving responsibility for different aspects of the plan to staff from different sections of the library, and bringing together people from other departments such as computing services, estates, finance and security to discuss it.

Whether or not the task of writing the disaster control plan should be the responsibility of a single member of staff or several, it was clear from many interviewees' comments that writing the disaster control plan is not a simple, straightforward task that can be readily given to junior members of staff with limited experience. One academic librarian, for example, explained that the task of devising her library's plan was initially given to a member of staff in their first professional post, but that it soon became apparent it should "become the responsibility of a senior member of staff". In particular, bringing together the various elements of the plan "necessitated liaison and negotiation with high level staff within and outside the organisation", and it was felt that this needed someone with the authority and confidence to make on the spot decisions at this level.

4.3.1.2 writing the disaster control plan

It was also clear from interviewees' comments that writing a disaster control plan can take a considerable amount of time, especially as it is unlikely that whoever is given the responsibility of writing the plan will be able to devote all of their time to doing so (that is, it will usually have to be undertaken along with their many other duties). Several librarians, therefore, found it beneficial to take what one described as a "step-by-step" approach, focusing on a particular aspect of the plan as and when they were able to do so. Similarly, another librarian, with considerable disaster management experience, advised that if it is not possible to complete the plan "all in one go" it may be necessary to "write a simple, basic plan...[and improve it]...as time allows".

A step-by-step approach may also be necessary because, not surprisingly, librarians often found themselves uncertain as to what should be included in the plan. There are, however, many published materials which may be consulted, and librarians who had consulted them found those items containing copies of other libraries' plans and guidelines on format and contents particularly useful. Disk versions of plans in wordprocessor format are also becoming more available for customisation by individual libraries. Details of these materials are included in the Bibliography at the end of the guidelines in part two.

Several other methods of obtaining information on writing a disaster control plan were recommended by interviewees, of which the most useful were considered to be making full use of any available in-house expertise (for example, consulting archivists and conservators), talking to other librarians who had written a plan of their own, attending seminars to listen to librarians, archivists and others with disaster experience and taking advice from external experts (for example, conservators, binders, salvage and restoration companies).

Nevertheless, although librarians should take full advantage of these and any other opportunities open to them, it is important to remember that each plan *must* be library, parent organisation and building specific. Each library must, therefore, draw up its own plan. Indeed, collecting the information required to write the plan, and then organising it and putting together as a plan, is itself an important part of the disaster management learning process.

4.3.2 Training

The importance of disaster management training at the preparedness stage was underlined by all interviewees, particularly, and significantly, by those with professional or personal disaster experience. A well-structured and targeted training programme was considered a vital prerequisite to a successful use of the written disaster control plan. In the words of one fire officer, for example, unless supported by training the plan will be "little more than words on paper". Disaster management training for *all* staff as appropriate should, therefore, be viewed as an integral aspect of good disaster management practice, not as something which may be 'added on' at a later date.

Unfortunately, several libraries visited experienced difficulties in obtaining the training they required, or obtaining it at a price they could afford. In one academic library, for example, training (seen as crucial by the librarian responsible for disaster management, and an activity which needed to be carried out before the library's written plan could be properly completed) had been delayed because the library could not find anybody who could offer the sort of practical training it wanted in-house. This is an issue which certainly requires further attention, and which might benefit from a more coordinated approach at regional and national levels.

4.3.2.1 training aims and objectives

We have already discussed the need to raise the awareness of *all* staff regarding the everyday safety and security of themselves and colleagues, users, collections, buildings, contents and facilities, and to highlight the steps they can take to reduce the likelihood of a disaster occurring. In addition, disaster management training must ensure that all staff know exactly what their own and their colleagues' roles and responsibilities will be in the event of a disaster. They should be made aware of the limitations of their own skills and knowledge and know when and where they should seek expert advice, for example, regarding conservation decisions.

It is also important to remember that disaster management is fundamentally about managing people. Therefore, as one interviewee from a commercial organisation with considerable disaster management training experience suggested, courses aimed at those with managerial roles such as Disaster Reaction Managers should include exercises to improve team building skills and provide an understanding of group dynamics.

4.3.2.2 training delivery

'Brainstorming' sessions were considered especially useful for bringing together library staff (of all grades) and staff from other sections and/or departments of the parent organisation. Ideally, this should happen before finalising the written disaster control plan and any other formal procedures. One library visited, for example, was about to hold a brainstorming exercise involving personnel from Computing and Telecoms, Collections and Preservation and House Management as part of a risk assessment exercise.

Practical workshops and advice on handling and sorting damaged materials will be necessary for Disaster Response Teams. Librarians and archivists suggested looking out for the one-day courses occasionally held by professional bodies such as the Institute of Paper Conservators, the Society of Archivists, Aslib and the Library Association, or contacting the commercial salvage and restoration companies who provide training, where in-house expertise is not available. Local fire authority officers may also be approached to participate in fire safety training exercises, for example, by being asked to give practical demonstrations in the correct use of fire extinguishers, although there may be charges for more in-depth training exercises. (The Oxford Colleges Conservation Consortium, for example, has paid the Oxfordshire Fire Service for practical training sessions involving entering and negotiating a smoke-filled room, and selecting and using the correct type of fire extinguisher on different types of fire.)

Disaster simulation exercises, however, were said by the majority of interviewees, including those with considerable experience as trainers in salvage companies and fire services, to be the most effective form of training (apart from involvement in a real disaster, though this was not recommended!). Not only are they essential in order to find out whether or not emergency procedures and instructions included in written disaster control plans will work in a real-life situation, they also give staff a better idea of what they can expect in various disaster scenarios such as fire and flood.

Several organisations visited had carried out disaster simulation exercises with great success, often discovering quite serious problems or omissions relating to their disaster preparedness and ability to cope in a real situation. They were then able to amend their plans or adapt their preparations based on what they had found. For example, an experienced disaster management trainer described how during an exercise in one organisation she visited, three people cut their hands on the sharp edges of a disaster trolley which had been bought to keep their emergency equipment and supplies on; a fire-officer described how during an exercise at a country house it was found that a plastic book-chute would not work when it rained; and, an archivist described how an exercise inside a large darkened building highlighted the need for hazard-tape to be kept as emergency equipment so that a 'one-way' system could be set up to prevent people bumping into each other. Similarly, a 'desktop exercise' at one major library, which included representatives from the emergency services, highlighted the need for someone from the library with a good knowledge of the building and its systems to remain on the scene to advise and accompany the fire officer-in-charge as necessary.

Problems such as these may only be discovered before a real disaster occurs by carrying out realistic simulations. Unfortunately, despite the overwhelmingly positive views of those involved in the above exercises, "the most useful of all" training initiatives being a typical comment, there was little evidence of any widespread use of them in libraries.

Although this is perhaps understandable - even those carrying out such training described it as difficult to organise and involving a lot of staff time - it does serve to underline the need for more disaster management training in libraries generally. As one conservator put it when asked how often staff receive disaster management training, "As in most institutions, not often enough. It should always be more than we give at present."

4.3.2.3 targeting training

Other than in very small libraries, not all staff will be heavily involved in disaster management, either before or after a disaster has occurred. Therefore, training will need to be targeted at particular individuals and groups according to their roles, responsibilities and level of involvement (taking due account of any relevant individual experience and expertise). Disaster Managers, Disaster Reaction Managers, Disaster Recovery Managers and members of Disaster Response Teams will all need to be targeted and their training needs assessed.

Of those requiring more in-depth training, however, the person(s) responsible for writing the library's disaster control plan will need to be targeted first as the training needs of those chosen to implement the plan and the skills they will need to do so will largely depend on how the plan is formulated.

4.3.3 Advice, expertise and services

Although they should always make full use of any available in-house expertise, libraries will still need to make prior arrangements for obtaining external advice, expertise and services which may be required following a disaster depending upon the given situation. The range of skills and services which may be needed is considerable and a list of sources which libraries should consider are contained in the guidelines in part two in the section on Preparedness.

Some advice, expertise and services may be available in-house, some may be offered free by fellow professionals in other libraries or archives and some will be offered on a commercial basis; this will largely depend upon the size and type of library and its parent organisation. Libraries need to be particularly careful when approaching outside individuals or companies. Interviewees stressed the need to be very specific when requesting details of the advice and services they can offer both to ensure that they meet their requirements and that any agreements or contracts entered into specifically cover the areas in question. They also stressed the fact that some 'advice' and 'services' may be offered for purely commercial reasons rather than in the best interests of the library. Libraries should, therefore, only approach reputable individuals and companies such as those well-known within the profession or with proven track records, and ask for a clear indication of their charges.

4.3.4 Emergency equipment and supplies

All the disaster recovery experts interviewed said that libraries should keep their own basic stocks of emergency equipment and supplies such as mops and buckets, torches, protective clothing, blotting paper and polythene sheeting for use if needed in the event of a disaster. What items of emergency equipment and supplies individual libraries decide to keep, and how much or how many of each, will depend upon factors such as the size of the library and the nature and value of its collections and whether or not some items are already held centrally within the parent organisation.

For immediate use, some emergency equipment and supplies may be kept on mobile 'disaster trolleys' - the Manchester Metropolitan University library, for example, uses a 'wheelie-bin', while the rest may be kept in storage. (Appendix H contains a list of items of emergency equipment and supplies libraries should consider holding.) Libraries, however, will also need to know where they can obtain more equipment and supplies quickly should they require them in an emergency and where they can hire larger or more expensive items of equipment such as dehumidifiers (some libraries may, of course, decide to keep their own dehumidifiers, after considering the above factors).

Whatever equipment and supplies they decide to keep, libraries must take care of them. For example, it is important to check that equipment is maintained in good working order and that supplies are not kept past any 'sell by date'.

4.3.4.1 cooperative initiatives

Libraries may wish to consider cooperative initiatives such as maintaining supplies of emergency equipment and supplies on a regional basis. For example, the East Midlands Museums Services' Regional Emergency and Disasters Squad (REDS), in addition to keeping centrally-held equipment and supplies, keeps stocks for immediate use in a series of small bags, designed to fit into the back of a saloon car, in each of its five counties. These stockpiles are intended to provide the Squad with basic equipment for rapid initial use during an emergency response, with individual organisations being expected to provide their own bulk supplies as necessary.

4.3.5 Insurance

Insurers rarely deal directly with librarians when preparing estimates or policies as parent organisations, whether local authorities, universities or businesses, usually have block policies which cover risks throughout the whole organisation, and which are the responsibility of insurance departments or sections in finance departments. This presented difficulties for some librarians interviewed who needed insurance information to formulate a coherent and meaningful disaster management strategy.

One librarian, for example, was "not allowed to see insurance policy documents or know details of cover". Another librarian found her finance department "reticent" about aspects of insurance such as the names of the insurers and the risks covered, and merely "received an assurance" that the library was adequately covered. A third librarian experienced similar reticence and was again "assured" that cover was "adequate".

Fortunately, interviewees who contacted insurers themselves found them to be extremely helpful. One insurance company, for example, "responded positively to queries about coverage...[for specific instances]...in the event of a disaster".

Certainly there appears to be a need for greater cooperation and understanding from some finance departments; at the very least librarians should be able to find out what cover they have for replacing lost or damaged items and providing any necessary temporary services. One answer may be for the library to demonstrate to its finance department just how seriously an interruption of its services could impact on the organisation as a whole. Alternatively, the library could highlight the value of its collections and point out how much it would cost to replace them or carry out conservation work in the event of a serious disaster. As one of the librarians experiencing difficulties obtaining information said, "this will probably surprise them".

Nevertheless, as interviewees with experience of insurance or loss adjustment pointed out, many librarians simply do not know the value of their collections, or, as one put it "even what is in them". Libraries need to address this issue, and, at the very least should have particularly important items valued, or in the case of

30

irreplaceable items, obtain estimates for any conservation work which may be necessary.

4.3.5.1 catalogues and inventories

As one insurance expert said, "a basic tenet of insurance is that the insured must prove loss". Insurers, therefore, strongly recommend that libraries keep up to date and comprehensive catalogues of their collections. They also recommend that libraries keep up to date and comprehensive inventories of contents such as office equipment and furniture.

As well as helping to establish proof of loss to insurers (and any agents acting for them such as loss adjusters), catalogues and inventories are likely to prove extremely useful when trying to rebuild collections or replace equipment and furnishings following a more serious incident. One interviewee, for example, described a situation in which it took several months to reconstruct documents and other items charred in a fire in order to identify them and put together a list of items lost. Indeed, the fact that their catalogue was one of the items lost, underlines the need for copies of both catalogues and inventories to be kept in separate locations outside the library.

4.3.6 Service continuity and access

Following a disaster the library may need to take steps to minimise any consequent effects on user services and to ensure users still have access to these services. Although it is obviously not possible to foresee exactly what will be needed following a particular incident, many interviewees, especially those with disaster experience, said that libraries should at least try to find suitable alternative accommodation from which to run temporary services should it be required and space in which to store temporarily any large quantities of stock which may need to be removed from the library. They should also consider cooperative initiatives with other libraries. Several London University college libraries, for example, have reciprocal arrangements regarding student access to important collections.

Interviewees did admit, however, that the situation regarding available accommodation could change at any time. Nevertheless, one interviewee described how a lack of prearranged temporary storage space "could have led to serious problems" following one major incident had a sympathetic local businessman not made surplus warehouse space available. He suggested that a centrally-held database of 'spare' accommodation, regularly updated, would have been very useful.

As several interviewees pointed out, libraries should make sure that they are covered for any 'consequential losses' incurred as a direct result of a disaster, and be aware of how long this cover will last following the disaster. Consequential loss will cover the library for costs such as loss of revenue from any charged-for services, temporary storage and accommodation, salvage operations and overtime payments. Libraries should be aware, however, that consequential loss cover does not include the cost of actually making a claim and that following a serious disaster this can be very expensive and time consuming (for example, somebody has to gather and put together the information necessary to make the claim while finance departments may have to process many hundreds of additional invoices).

4.4 Reaction

Reaction involves raising the alarm, evacuating the building, instigating initial procedures and activities aimed at protecting undamaged materials, salvaging damaged materials and stabilising the environment.

This section will consider:

- taking expert advice
- communication
- human resources
- health and safety
- keeping a record
- dealing with the media

4.4.1 Taking expert advice

Following a disaster, the overwhelming message from interviewees was if in any doubt, take expert advice, especially when handling and sorting damaged or threatened valuable items. Indeed we have already discussed the importance of identifying conservation expertise in advance as part of disaster preparedness activities. Several interviewees, however, described incidents which further underline its importance.

One company specialising in salvage and restoration work, for example, was asked by a university library to collect and defrost antiquarian and archive materials which, according to the library, were "O.K." as it had managed to "freeze them quickly". Unfortunately, defrosting only revealed the extent to which the items were badly damaged and contaminated, damage and contamination which should have been dealt with immediately before it got worse. In another incident a salvage and restoration expert was called to a library which had suffered a serious fire. She found that tightly-shelved books which had become wet during fire-fighting had been damaged still further because one had been removed to assess the damage causing them all to expand and buckle.

This is not to suggest that reacting quickly is not important; "Stabilizing wet materials as quickly as possible is essential for successful recovery" (Buchanan, 1988, p. 77), while following a fire "It is very important that the book cleaning should start as soon as possible. The longer that the books are left soiled the more intensive the treatment becomes to restore them" (Thorburn, 1993, p. 76). It is simply to suggest that "It is worth spending time to assess the damage and situation and to brief teams. Time so spent will be more than saved by the orderly and informed approach that should follow" (McIntyre, 1989, p. 6). Comments from interviewees, for example, included "Stop and think", "Take a calm coordinated approach" and "Try not to rush. Things often look bad, but you may have more time...[to put things right]...than you realise".

Interviewees also stressed the fact that it is important to remember that each of the organisations on the library's list of emergency contacts will have its own area(s) of expertise and skill. A disaster recovery expert, for example, described how during a particular incident one company did "an excellent job" of sorting out casual labour and emergency equipment, but was not so good at "more delicate operations such as clearing up afterwards", while another which took care of book cleaning, was "better at listening" and "less destructive"!

Remember also that a disaster may attract all kinds of vested interests. Libraries should, for example, be wary of industrial cleaners offering to undertake tasks such as cleaning smoke-damaged books or computers. These and other specialist tasks should be left to organisations competent in these areas and with proven track records.

Choosing the right company for a specific task will be far less of a problem if the library already has a properly compiled and comprehensive list of sources of advice, expertise and services. The different types of sources of advice, expertise and services which libraries should consider contacting and compiling lists of in advance are included in part two in the section on Preparedness.

4.4.1.1 library expertise
In certain circumstances, for example, if a loss is likely to be over a certain amount, insurers will bring in loss adjusters part of whose job is to take actions to mitigate the loss. The loss adjusters acting as 'honest brokers' may in turn bring in various salvage and conservation experts. In this type of situation many decisions may be taken out of the hands of library managers.

Whatever the situation, however, librarians have their own professional expertise and must always make sure that they are consulted before any action is taken. Otherwise, insurers, loss-adjusters or non-library managers within the parent organisation may get together and arrange to have something done which to

34

them seems practical and sensible, but which may have serious consequences for the library. One salvage expert, for example, described how in one school the Head of the Board of Governors brought in volunteers to pack smoke-damaged items for removal. They simply put items into boxes haphazardly with no thought of where they came from in the library; having no library background, they did not appreciate that the collection was classified and needed to be re-shelved exactly as before.

4.4.2 Communication

Cooperation between all interested parties, particularly following a more serious disaster, is crucial to effective disaster reaction and recovery just as it is essential to have a centralised, coordinated approach. Everyone needs to be working towards the same goals and to appreciate how these goals can best be achieved. This will not be possible unless people talk to each other and understand each other's needs and problems. As one disaster recovery expert said the security manager may "see" an open window which needs to be boarded up to stop people getting into the building, whereas the Disaster Recovery Manager "sees" the only source of light and ventilation.

One interviewee with considerable salvage experience recommended that a team representing all interested parties should be set up immediately following a serious incident and that this team should spend "a couple of hours" formulating a coherent, structured plan which is then managed centrally by a recognised authority. The team should meet regularly throughout the disaster response so that team members can see what action has been taken since their last meeting and raise any problems which they believe require attention.

Unfortunately, communication problems, leading to considerable frustration and delay, were often highlighted by interviewees as causing the most trouble following a disaster. These problems were also said to increase dramatically following a large scale incident. For instance, minor damage caused by a burst radiator in a branch library can be handled fairly easily by the library service, whereas an incident such as the Norwich Central Library fire immediately becomes a 'county council' rather than a 'library' problem.

This underlines once more the need for the library to build up good working relationships with other departments and sections within its parent organisation throughout the disaster management process and certainly before an incident actually occurs. Establishing similar relationships with key individuals in external organisations such as emergency equipment suppliers and restoration and salvage companies can also help to promote communication and cooperation when it is needed most.

4.4.3 Human resources

We have already discussed the importance of having the right person in charge of disaster reaction and recovery and the qualities they require. Equally important is the enthusiasm and cooperation of Disaster Response Team members and any other staff who may become involved as the situation progresses. For example, one interviewee pointed out that it may not always be the most senior staff who "pull everything together" citing a situation in which a clerical officer was largely responsible for organising and prioritising her department's disaster response while other, more senior, staff were often "too focused" in their approach.

Not surprisingly, then, many interviewees stressed the importance of maintaining staff morale, particularly following a more serious incident requiring a long and arduous response. Interviewees with disaster experience found that staff tended to be extremely willing and helpful during an initial disaster reaction, but warned that this enthusiasm could quickly dissipate if, to paraphrase many of their comments, staff felt that they were being taken for granted and their needs ignored.

4.4.4 Health and safety

All interviewees agreed that the health and safety of the public and staff must be the paramount concern during any disaster response. Following discovery of a serious fire, for instance, the library will be evacuated immediately and people will not be allowed to enter the building until given the 'all clear' by the emergency services.

There are, however, many basic health and safety issues which libraries need to be aware of even during a reaction to a relatively minor incident. Wet books, for example, are deceptively heavy, and carrying large quantities of them for any length of time is not only very tiring, it can also lead to back problems if they are not picked up, carried and put down properly. Indeed, one salvage expert suggested that it is probably better to keep back supports in emergency supplies rather than Wellington boots.

In addition, although most library managers and staff will at least be aware that there are problems associated with lifting heavy materials, many health and safety issues are not so obvious or well-understood. In fact several interviewees with considerable disaster experience said that they often found a significant lack of awareness regarding health and safety when called in to manage a disaster reaction. Not surprisingly, therefore, they believed health and safety to be an area in need of far greater attention. One, for example, suffered health problems which were found to be caused by dioxins leaking from a cadmium battery in a portable stereo which had been seriously damaged in a fire.

As one salvage and restoration expert has suggested, "There are far too many unanswered questions concerning the dangers in a building that has been heated to over 1,000 [degrees] C. Some believe that partially burnt toner from a photocopier could have adverse effects if contact is made with it. There is also considerable debate over the capacitors in fluorescent tubing, which may contain polychlorinated biphenyls (PCBs)" (Donnelly, 1992, p. 27). Harmful air pollution may, therefore, be caused by fire damage either to contents or to the fabric of the building. Thus, following a serious fire air quality needs to be tested and monitored regularly to determine whether or not the library is safe to work in. Indeed, even smaller fires may release particles hazardous to health, and rather than take risks libraries should always seek expert advice regarding air quality. In addition, data gathered from any testing and monitoring may be used to answer questions on air quality raised by staff at a later date.

Water may also be hazardous to health and safety. Once again, there is a more 'obvious' risk, that of electrocution, and others better known to the experts than the layperson such as bacterial contamination and the possibility that "Workers who enter a water damaged area without protective clothing may contract Weil's or other viral diseases" (Donnelly and Heaney, 1993, p. 71).

Furthermore, one disaster recovery expert pointed out that health and safety issues are strongly linked to staff morale. Hard hats, face masks, surgical gloves and overalls may be uncomfortable to wear, but, in addition to the protection they afford, staff can see that they are "being well looked after".

4.4.5 Keeping a record

The decisions and actions taken following any disaster no matter how small should be noted as they occur (before memory fails) and a report written up afterwards. Many of these decisions and actions may turn out to have been the right ones and it is important to know this for future reference. More significantly perhaps, mistakes may have been made and lessons must also be learned from these. Neither will be possible unless the decisions and actions taken, along with the reasons they were taken, have been accurately recorded for subsequent analysis. As one librarian with disaster experience said "[although time-consuming]...looking at what was done in a methodical way enables mistakes to be more easily identified and thus avoided in the future".

In addition, as several interviewees, including insurance experts, pointed out, disaster reports can be extremely useful when submitting insurance claims as the library's insurers (or loss adjusters acting on their behalf) may well want to know why certain decisions or actions were taken before settling the claim. Having to try to remember why these decision or actions were taken a later date is both open to error and may be considered unprofessional.

4.4.6 Dealing with the media

The overwhelming view among interviewees who had experience of dealing with the media (whether radio, television or newspapers) following a disaster was that it was very time consuming and deflected attention away from other more pressing activities. For example, in one library the senior officer in charge spent "far too much time talking to the media" which meant that he often had to delegate authority on an ad hoc basis as he was called away.

Dealing with the media was also described as being very stressful. Interviewees' comments included,"at first they may be 'friendly'...[but then they want]...somebody to blame", "[the press and other media]...are infuriating...[they]...will do anything to get a story", "[they are]...always looking for a 'good story'" and "Whatever happens the press are going to write a story".

Nevertheless, with hindsight, several interviewees believed that enquiries from the media could have been dealt with better than they were. First of all, it is extremely important to try to control the situation and all media enquiries should be directed to a single point of contact within the library, the Media Liaison Officer. This may not always be easy, however, and "although it is accepted wisdom that...[dealing with the media]...should be delegated, there is an insistence on getting the reaction of the person in charge" (Kennedy, 1995, p. 6). Staff must, in any case, be aware that they should never talk to the media themselves; as one experienced interviewee put it, although the media will start talking to those "at the top", they will work their way down "until they get a story."

Several interviewees also pointed out that the media, particularly local radio and newspapers, can be very helpful "if the library gets them on its side". They may, for example, assist in disseminating information on temporary and alternative service arrangements or, during the recovery stage, help with appeals to replace lost items of particular significance such as local history materials.

The Media Liaison Officer, therefore, needs to establish a rapport with the media, to be seen as the person who knows what is going on, and to be as helpful as possible in order to build up a good working relationship. For instance, as one interviewee pointed out, journalists work to strict deadlines (such as on the hour radio news bulletins, lunchtime and early evening television news programmes and newspaper print runs). The Media Liaison Officer by providing journalists with information in time to meet these deadlines will quickly be seen as an asset rather than as someone to be by-passed.

4.5 Recovery

Recovery involves post-reaction procedures and activities aimed at restoring buildings, collections, contents, facilities and services, and implementing any necessary measures to ensure service continuity and access.

This section will consider:

- service continuity and access
- conservation advice
- counselling
- reviewing the disaster control plan
- final recovery

4.5.1 Service continuity and access

Several interviewees emphasised that however serious a particular disaster may be for the library itself, life outside "goes on as normal". The public library's readers will still want to return and borrow books, the university's students will still need materials to help them complete assignments and the Managing Director will still want those latest economic indicators. The post - and any stationery, office equipment, books, periodicals and other stock items already ordered or on subscription - will be delivered as usual.

In addition, although the library's users and other departments and sections within the parent organisation may be quite sympathetic immediately following a disaster, many interviewees with disaster experience felt that this sympathy was likely to be fairly short-lived. In fact, libraries in commercial organisations may face considerable internal pressure to get back to normal as quickly as possible as failure to do so could lead to loss of business or, even to the collapse of the business; in a situation such as this the need to ensure service continuity suddenly becomes the need to ensure business continuity.

Just as worrying from the library's point of view, as one librarian pointed out, a library in a commercial organisation may be asked to reduce staff or even be threatened with closure if the business is seen to be "able to manage without it" for any length of time. Indeed, these threats could be said apply to any library in any organisation looking to make economies. Maintaining service continuity and access is, therefore, an issue of major importance.

Emergency arrangements made for setting up temporary services, accommodation and storage facilities should be implemented as prevailing circumstances demand. The situation can quickly change, however, and in the event of a more serious disaster maintaining service continuity and access will become the responsibility of the Disaster Recovery Manager. He or she will need to react to circumstances as they unfold, but with clearly defined aims and goals in mind. As one disaster recovery expert put it, the Disaster Recovery Manager "must be fully aware of what the library is trying to achieve...[and work]...flexibly, but resolutely, towards achieving these aims".

Attention will need to be given to how the short, medium and long term functions of the service can be managed. Appropriate management structures and teams with clearly defined responsibilities will need to be established. Ideally, two teams, each separately managed, should be assembled, one to set up and maintain temporary services and the other to deal with the disaster recovery itself. Where networked computer facilities are affected there will need to be close liaison with internal computer services departments or external service providers.

Several disaster recovery experts noted that whatever preparations have been made each disaster is unique and needs to be dealt with as effectively and as efficiently as possible by whoever is present using whatever resources are necessary. Nevertheless, they also pointed out that without these preparations there may be a far greater impact on services and access. Consequently, maintaining them also becomes that much more difficult. As with so many other aspects of reaction and recovery, preparation is crucial to a more efficient and effective response.

4.5.2 Conservation advice

All damaged items will either need to be discarded or sorted according to the type and scale of damage sustained so that any necessary conservation work can be carried out. This may involve work on single items that can be carried out immediately or longer term projects requiring careful management. Again interviewees stressed that where any doubts exist actions should be based on the advice of the experts already identified in the disaster control plan. Unfortunately, (and once again) libraries were often offered conflicting advice on conservation issues leaving difficult decisions still to be made regarding the best course of action to be taken. This was so, for instance, when it came to deciding which items needed to be frozen.

Freezing, and thereby stabilising, wet materials which cannot be dealt with immediately is generally recommended "because of the need to avoid making hasty and bad decisions about a collection which is likely to be a variety of materials and complex structures" (McIntyre, 1989, p. 7). Following one disaster, however, a library was advised by conservators to put wet books into plastic bags for freezing only to be informed a little while later by a salvage expert that they would have dried out "in a matter of minutes" if fanned and left to dry "naturally" as the weather was so warm. While in a similar situation, a conservator advised that certain valuable materials should not be frozen as they would be damaged, whereas the salvage company's project manager advised that they should be frozen as soon as possible to stabilise them before mould developed.

Several librarians were also confused about the use of freeze drying and vacuum drying in the treatment of wet materials. For example, are they relatively expensive treatments which should only be used to salvage antiquarian or valuable irreplaceable items? Can only paper-based materials be treated using these processes, or are they suitable for other materials such as parchment or leather? What sort of condition will the items be returned in? How long will it be before the items are returned? Although there may not be simple 'right' or 'wrong' answers regarding such issues, the findings at the very least suggest that more information is needed in non-technical language that librarians can understand.

4.5.3 Counselling

Interviewees with disaster experience invariably felt that the physical and mental stress which staff can suffer as the result of even a relatively minor disaster is generally underestimated; as one of them said, "a disaster does not have to be of Norwich proportions to be traumatic". Several also pointed out that while no organisation can provide a high standard of service for any length of time without enthusiastic and well-motivated staff under normal circumstances, it becomes quite impossible following a disaster. It is, therefore, essential that counselling be made available to all staff and members of their families.

Librarians with disaster experience said they were surprised at how emotionally attached they and their staff had become to their library and its collections. They also pointed out how unsettling a disruption to normal working routines can be for some staff, especially if they are feeling insecure about their jobs. Relocated staff in particular may find working in strange environments with different people stressful, while temporary accommodation may be cramped and far from ideal. This stress may not be confined to those who have been relocated, however, and such a move may be extremely disruptive to those whose space is 'invaded'. One librarian, for instance, described how, during a temporary relocation of the library, the continual ringing of the library's telephone upset other workers whose telephones usually rang only once or twice an hour.

On the other hand, several interviewees said that it is important to appreciate that for some people being involved in a serious disaster and its aftermath will have been one of the most exciting periods of their lives. As one salvage expert remarked, "it's a long way down even to get back to normal everyday emotional levels".

Counselling is thus not something that should be offered to staff for the first few days after the disaster and then forgotten about. One librarian, for example, said that although she did not take up the offer of counselling immediately after her library's disaster she has since felt that it would have been beneficial as it was around two months before she could really talk about the incident "without tears". Another librarian had "never taken so much sick leave" in her life, while a third said that she would be taking a day's leave on the anniversary of a disaster in her library as she could not face coming in on that day.

Furthermore, the offer of counselling should not be dependent on the status of staff. One interviewee described how following one incident counselling was offered to all permanent staff, but was not made available to relief library and information assistants, one of whom would "certainly have benefited from it".

Nevertheless, as one disaster recovery expert stressed, although counselling should be made available to all staff who want it, there is much that can be done to "keep spirits up" on a day to day basis during the recovery period. Maintaining a teamwork approach at all times and getting staff together at the beginning and end of each day to discuss progress and allow them to raise any problems and concerns which they might have can be particularly helpful in this regard.

4.5.4 Reviewing the written disaster control plan

We have already noted the importance and benefits of keeping a record of what was done following any disaster, no matter how small, and writing up a report afterwards. These reports should also be used as the basis for reviewing the written disaster control plan to see whether or not it requires amendment or revision. (Other circumstances requiring review of the plan are highlighted in the guidelines in part two.) Although this may seem obvious in the case of a serious disaster, even minor disasters which are dealt with swiftly and effectively with very little effort can give warning of unforeseen and potentially more serious risks, or suggest ways in which the plan could be improved upon.

4.5.5 Final recovery

"It's important to appreciate how long it takes to get back to normal". This was a comment from a librarian who had experienced a particularly serious disaster, but it was a comment made by many other interviewees with experience of disasters both 'large' and 'small'. For example, one flood-damaged library originally assumed that it would need temporary storage facilities for about three months during refurbishment, whereas it was eventually needed for ten months. Similarly, replacing damaged office equipment such as computers may take a lot longer than expected. It may also be a considerable amount of time before office equipment sent for cleaning is returned, and in many cases individual items will come back in "dribs and drabs" as one librarian put it.

All this inevitably leads to frustration. Frustration "in not being able to get things done quickly or efficiently, frustration at the apparent incompetence of the supposed experts, and frustration in not being able to offer the expected service to your customers" (Green, p. 75).

More positively, libraries experiencing disasters - even serious ones - have recovered from them (see, for example, Davies, 1995 and Saunders, 1993); the library can, and will, survive. Librarians may even return to find a better library than the one they had before - although nobody has suggested going through the pain and trauma of a major disaster in order to achieve this! Lessons will have been learned and loss adjusters and insurers, according to several interviewees, will often listen sympathetically to suggestions for refurbishment which include upgrading environmental conditions or installing new safety features to provide better protection for the library and its collections in the future. Indeed, it is in the interests of both the library and its insurers that any work which may reduce the likelihood of a further disaster is carried out.

5. Summary and recommendations

This research has drawn on the practical experience and expertise of librarians and others with a wide range of specialist skills and knowledge in different aspects of disaster management. The main findings have been highlighted and discussed in this report. Specific recommendations for library managers dealing with disaster management on a day to day basis are incorporated in the guidelines which follow the report. The recommendations below are intended for broader professional attention.

Awareness raising and discussion

The National Preservation Office has already established a key role in this area and with other professional bodies and other interested parties should continue to promote good practice and debate. The following issues would benefit from further promotion and professional discussion:

- the importance and application of risk assessment to effective disaster management
- the feasibility of installing modern fire detection and suppression systems.

It is important that technical issues are addressed in language which makes them understandable to library managers.

The development of a British based World Wide Web site for preservation with links to web sites abroad should be considered for the further promotion and discussion of preservation issues, including disaster management.

Broader professional involvement and cooperation

Disaster management is currently of wide interest not only to librarians, but also to others working in related fields such as archives, heritage and museums. Some cooperative ventures have already taken place. More should be encouraged to exploit common ground and to maintain the current momentum. A national seminar to be attended by representatives of professional bodies and other interested parties, might be a particularly useful way forward.

Disaster management advice, expertise and services

Libraries need to be confident that the sources of advice, expertise and services they choose are going to be efficient, effective and reliable when needed. The feasibility of having a national register of such sources compiled and held by a disinterested third party should be considered. Companies and services active in disaster management might also consider developing an agreed set of standards against which services and products could be assessed. Initial consideration of these could be made at the seminar suggested above.

Research

The following areas might benefit from further investigation:

- Health and Safety issues. For example, what are the carcinogenic effects of particles remaining in the atmosphere following fire damage to plastic equipment such as photocopiers? Are staff fully aware of the dangers of contracting infections from contaminated water? Research into these may have already been carried out, if so it needs to be identified and explained in a way that is clear to librarians

- Salvage and conservation. A comparative study of different salvage procedures and conservation treatments might help librarians decide between the options available to them. Such a study would look at the effects of each type of treatment on individual items and associated costs.

Training

The professional bodies have a considerable role to play in facilitating training opportunities for libraries which have little or no recourse to in house expertise. Topics which should be addressed include:

- conservation treatments
- dealing with the media
- recognising risks to buildings, collections, contents and facilities
- salvaging damaged materials
- valuing and insuring collections.

Emphasis should be on the practical, with a 'hands-on' approach.

Libraries should look for local or regional partners with whom they can share costs, expertise and facilities; they may also like to consider offering places to those outside their organisations to subsidise training costs.

6. References

Anderson, Hazel and McIntyre, John E. 1985. *Planning manual for disaster control in Scottish libraries and record offices.* Edinburgh: National Library of Scotland.

Brown, Ian. 1994. Sprinkler systems for public sector buildings: the facts and the fictions. *Public Sector Risk!*, 5, pp. 7-8.

Buchanan, Sally. 1988. *Disaster planning, preparedness and recovery for libraries and archives: a RAMP study with guidelines.* (PGI-88/WS/6). Paris: General Information Programme and UNISIST, United Nations Educational, Scientific and Cultural Organisation.

Butler, Randall. 1986. The Los Angeles Central Library fire. *Conservation Administration News*, 27, October, pp. 1-2, 23-24.

Donnelly, Helene. 1992. Saving library collections. *Fire Prevention*, 254, November, pp. 26-27.

Donnelly, Helene and Heaney, Martin. 1993. Disaster planning - a wider approach. *Aslib Information*, 21(2), February, pp. 69-71.

Eden, Paul, Feather, John and Matthews, Graham. 1994. Preservation and library management: a reconsideration. *Library Management*, 15(4), pp. 5-11.

Feather, John, Matthews, Graham and Eden, Paul. 1996. *Preservation management: policies and practices in British libraries.* Aldershot: Gower.

Fire rekindles debate. 1994. *Library Association Record*, 96(9), September, p. 69.

Green, Kevin. 1993. The case of the Pilkington Technology Centre fire. *Aslib Information*, 21(2), February, pp. 72-75.

Hyams, David. 1993. *The guide to disaster recovery planning.* Oxford: MRC Business Information Group.

Kennedy, Jean. 1995. Norfolk Record Office fire: an initial report. *Journal of the Society of Archivists*, 16(1), pp. 3-6.

Matthews, Graham. 1988. Fire and water damage at the USSR Academy of Sciences Library, Leningrad, *Library Association Record*, 90(5), May, pp. 279-281.

McIntyre, J.E. 1989. Action planning for disaster. *Refer*, 5(4), Autumn, pp. 1-7.

Municipal Mutual. 1991. *Museum protection. A practical guide.* London: Municipal Mutual Insurance Ltd.

National Preservation Office. 1988. *If disaster strikes!* London: NPO. (Videocassette.)

National Preservation Office/Riley Dunn and Wilson. 1989. *Keeping our words: the 1988 National Preservation Office Competition [disaster control planning]: the winning entry and two 'Highly Commended' entries.* London: NPO.

Pearson, B.P. 1995. *An inquiry into the fire at the Norwich Central Library on the 1st August 1994.* Norwich:

Norfolk County Council. (The Pearson Report.)

Saunders, Margaret. 1993. How a library picked up the pieces after IRA blast. *Library Association Record*, 95(2), February, pp. 100-101.

Stimpson, Alan. 1994. Protecting special places - the Intelligent Sprinkler. *Public Sector Risk!*, 5, pp. 9-10.

Thorburn, Georgine. 1993. Library fire and flood - successful salvage, but beware of the cowboy. *Aslib Information*, 21(2), February, pp.76-78.

Tregarthen Jenkin, Ian. 1987. *Disaster planning and preparedness: an outline disaster control plan.* London: British Library. (British Library Information Guide 5.)

Wise, Christine. 1995. The flood and afterwards: a new beginning for the Fawcett Library. *Library Conservation News*, 48, Autumn, pp. 1-2.

Appendix A. Letter to libraries requesting a copy of their written disaster control plan

{name & address}

5th April 1995

Dear {name}

DISASTER MANAGEMENT IN BRITISH LIBRARIES

Since the fire and destruction at Norwich Central Library in August last year, there has been keen demand from library managers for up to date advice and guidelines on best practice for disaster management. In May 1993, your library kindly replied to our questionnaire survey on Preservation policy and management, which included a question about disaster control planning. Building on this earlier research, we are now working on a British Library Research and Development Department funded project investigating current disaster management practice. We are writing to all libraries who replied to our earlier survey saying that they had a disaster control plan.

The 1993 survey found that only 30% of the libraries that responded had a disaster control plan. A key factor in our present research is the analysis of existing disaster control plans. We would be most grateful, therefore, if you could send us a copy of your library's disaster control plan. It is not our intention to criticise individual library's disaster control plans. Rather, we wish to identify common, core features and to look for unique aspects which might be of broader application. All plans and any additional information received will be treated in confidence.

One of the outcomes of this research will be the production of recommended guidelines for disaster prevention and management based on best practice. Information gathered from the analysis of disaster control plans will be a key factor in the compilation of these guidelines. Whilst it is impossible to remove totally the incidence of disasters in libraries, sharing experience and expertise may help to minimise their frequency and effect.

Please send a copy of your library's disaster control plan to Paul Eden, Research Associate, at the above address. (Postage will be refunded if requested.) Should you have any queries, Paul can be contacted on 01509 223098; e-mail: P.Eden@uk.ac.lut

The project has the support of the National Preservation Office, based at the British Library.

Once again, many thanks for your time and co-operation, we hope you will be able to help us.

Yours sincerely,

Graham Matthews
Project Head

Appendix B. List of libraries and archives sending a copy of their written disaster control plan

University libraries:

Aberdeen

Bristol

Cambridge

Cambridge, Emmanuel

Cambridge, Institute of Education

Cambridge, St John's

Central Lancashire

De Montfort

East Anglia

Glasgow

Glasgow Caledonian

Hull

Keele

Lancaster

London, Imperial College of Science, Technology and Medicine

London, Institute of Classical Studies

London, King's

London, School of African and Oriental Studies

London, St Mary's Hospital Medical School

Manchester Metropolitan

Manchester

Newcastle

Northumbria

Oxford, Faculty of Music

Oxford, Magdalen

Oxford, New College

Oxford, St Edmund

Southampton

Wales, College of Medicine

Warwick

Total number of academic libraries = 30

Public libraries:

Calderdale Central Library

Dunfermline Libraries and Museums

East Lothian Libraries and Museums

East Sussex Libraries

Essex County Libraries

Newcastle upon Tyne Libraries and Arts

Northamptonshire Libraries and Information Service

South Eastern Education and Library Board, Library and Information Service (NI)

Warwickshire County Library Service

Total number of public libraries = 9

National/special libraries and archives:

British Architectural Library

British Film Institute

British Library

British Medical Association

Cheshire Record Office

Chetham's Library

Commercial Union

Hereford Cathedral

House of Lords

Institute of Chartered Accountants in England and Wales

Ipswich Institute

Law Society

Linnean Society

Ministry of Agriculture and Fisheries

National Art Library

National Library of Scotland

National Library of Wales

Public Record Office

Royal Commission on the Historical Monuments of England

Royal Entomological Society

Royal Society

Selly Oak Colleges

Suffolk Record Office

Walsall Local History Centre

Total number of national/special libraries and archives = 24

Total number of written disaster control plans received = 63

DISASTER MANAGEMENT IN BRITISH LIBRARIES

British Library Research and Development Department Funded Project

Graham Matthews and Paul Eden
Department of Information and Library Studies, Loughborough University

Semi-structured interview schedule

Interviewee(s):

Position(s):

Organisation:

**We fully appreciate the sensitive nature of some of the questions we are asking.
All information will be treated in the strictest confidence**

1. Do you have a Disaster Control Plan?
YES/NO

If yes,

a) Is the DCP a written plan?
YES/NO

b) Is the DCP available in electronic format?
YES/NO

c) When was the DCP formulated?

d) How often is the DCP up-dated?

e) What instigated the writing of the DCP?

f) Who devised the DCP? [If the DCP was devised by someone within the organisation, but outside
the library, what input did the library have?]

g) How long did it take to produce the DCP?

h) If you devised the plan, in what areas was your own knowledge most deficient?

i) What sources (for example, documents or other organisations) were most useful in the formulation of the DCP?

j) For which area(s) of the DCP was there a shortage of available information?

k) For which area(s) of the DCP was it necessary to bring in outside expertise?

l) Does the DCP include computer hardware, software and systems?
YES/NO

If no, how are these dealt with?

m) Were risk assessments carried out?
YES/NO

If yes, who carried them out and what areas/functions/systems were assessed?

n) What were the financial implications of drawing up and providing the necessary resources for effective implementation of the DCP [that is, what additional funding was needed]?

o) Does the DCP cover more than one site/location?
YES/NO

If yes, please give details

p) If you do not have a DCP is this because of practical constraints such as lack of time, staff or knowledge, or has it not been considered necessary?

2. **Who has overall responsibility for disaster management/the DCP and why were they chosen?**

3. **Is someone separately responsible for computer security/disaster control planning?**
YES/NO

If yes, please give details

4. **Do you have any provisions for training staff in aspects of disaster management (for example, disaster prevention or what to do during a disaster)?**
YES/NO

If yes,

a) What training is there (for example, drills, simulations)?

b) Who is trained?

c) How often is training given?

d) Who does the training?

e) How is training validated?

5. Does the library have fire detection and/or suppression systems?
   YES/NO

If yes, please give details

6. Is the library and/or its collections insured?
   YES/NO

If yes,

a) What type of insurance is it?

b) Which company are you insured with?

c) What is the extent of the insurance coverage?

d) [If applicable] does having a disaster plan significantly reduce insurance premiums?

7. How have Health and Safety issues relating to the library been addressed?

8. Have you had any disasters over the last five years?
   YES/NO

If yes,

a) Please give details [including which company/ies carried out salvage and recovery]

b) Was a DCP implemented during the disaster?
YES/NO

If no, would there have been any advantages in having a DCP at the time of the disaster(s)?

c) What were the key problems you experienced during any disasters and their aftermath?

i) during

ii) after

d) [If applicable] In what way(s) did any disasters affect review of the DCP?

e) With hindsight, what, if anything, would you have done differently during any disasters or their aftermath?

9. What preventive measures have been taken in order to minimise the risk of any future disasters? [Which, if any, of these have been driven by legal considerations?]

10. Is the library a member of any cooperative disaster management scheme?
YES/NO

a) If yes, please give details

b) If no, do you have any back-up arrangements with any other organisations?

c) Does business confidentiality impair such arrangements? YES/NO

If yes, in what ways?

11. What 3 key pieces of advice would you give to anyone facing a disaster situation?

12. What key skills/attributes do you think anyone facing a disaster situation needs?

13. Any other comments?

Many thanks for your time and cooperation

Appendix D. List of interviewees and organisations visited

John Baldwin. Risk and Insurance Manager, *Norfolk County Council*

Nancy Bell. Conservation Officer, *Magdalen College, Oxford/Oxford Colleges Conservation Consortium*

Bill Bennett. Support Services Officer/Divisional Officer, *Norfolk Fire Service*

Tina Brooks. Community Librarian, *Sheffield Libraries and Information Services*

Vic Brown. Managing Director, *Imbach RAG*

Mike Burrows. Sales Development Manager, *Munters Moisture Control Services*

Maureen Castens. Head of Library Services, *London Guildhall University*

Wayne Connolly. Hollings Site Librarian, *Manchester Metropolitan University*

Neal Courtney. Sales and Marketing Director, *Imbach RAG*

Edward Diestelkamp. Adviser on Architecture, *The National Trust*

Helene Donnelly. Founder, *Data and Archival Damage Control Centre*

Sue Donnelly. Assistant Archivist, *British Library of Political and Economic Science*

Charles Dunn. Sales and Marketing Director, *Riley Dunn and Wilson*

Lynn Elliott. Deputy Librarian, Head of Technical Services, *Manchester Metropolitan University*

Andrew Fletcher. Senior Librarian, *Sheffield Libraries and Information Services*

Helen Forde. Head of Preservation Services, *Public Record Office*

Kevin Fromings. Executive Officer, *British Library, Collections and Preservation*

Terry Glossop. Chief Fire Officer, *Gwent Fire Brigade* and Chairman, *Chief and Assistant Chief Fire Officers'*
   Association, Fire Safety Committee

Ken Gibbons. Assistant Librarian, *British Library of Political and Economic Science*

Robert Hales. Managing Director, *Cedric Chivers*

John Handey. Senior Divisional Officer, *Nottinghamshire Fire and Rescue Service*

David Hayman. Assistant Director, Disaster Recovery, *Norfolk Library and Information Service*

Adrian Henstock. Principal Archivist, *Nottinghamshire Archives*

David Hyams. Consultant Architect, *Building Information*

Alan Johnston. Principal Museums Officer, *Hampshire County Council Museums Service*

Jean Kennedy. County Archivist, *Norfolk County Record Office*

John Lake. Principal Library Manager, *East Sussex Library Service, Brighton Area Libraries*

David Lathrope. Assistant Director, *Leisure Services/Libraries, Nottinghamshire County Council*

David Leech. Senior Loss Control Surveyor, *Zurich Municipal, Zurich Insurance Company*

Ron Leith. Director, *McLarens Chartered Loss Adjusters*

Nick London. Principal Systems Officer, *County Library Support Services, Nottinghamshire County Council*

John McIntyre. Head of Preservation, *National Library of Scotland*

Ken McKenzie. Managing Director, *Harwell Drying Restoration Services*

Robin Millest. Director, *Imbach RAG*

Tom Moulton, Security Manager, St. Pancras Project, *British Library*

Theresa Mowah. Higher Executive Officer, *British Library, Collections and Preservation*

Ian Murray, Lecturer, *Department of Information and Library Studies, Loughborough University*

Barry Ockleford. Fire Safety Adviser, *English Heritage*

Karen Plouviez. House Manager, St. Pancras, *British Library*

Russell Pocock. Sales and Marketing Director, *Cedric Chivers*

Linda Ramsey. Conservation Manager, *Scottish Record Office*

Fergus Read. (then) Assistant Director, *East Midlands Museums Service* and Coordinator, *Regional Emergencies and Disaster Squad (REDS)*

Dorothy Russell. Senior Library and Information Assistant, *Sheffield Libraries and Information Services*

Margaret Saunders. Group Librarian, *Commercial Union Asset Management*

Barbara Sharp. Senior Archivist, Archive Services, *Nottinghamshire Archives*

Larry Stokes. Underwriting Manager, *Zurich Municipal, Zurich Insurance Company*

Bill Stolworthy. Assistant Director, *Management, Property Strategy Group, Norfolk County Council*

Georgine Thorburn. Managing Director, *Document SOS*

Mats Tykesson. Divisional Manager, *Munters Moisture Control Services*

Maureen Wade. Sub-Librarian (Technical Services), *British Library of Political and Economic Science*

Christine Wise. Fawcett Development Librarian, *Fawcett Library, London Guildhall University*

John Woodhouse. Head of Bookbinding and Conservation, *John Rylands University Library of Manchester*

Graham Wray. Estates Manager, *Property Strategy Group, Norfolk County Council*

The following also gave us advice:

John Hodgson. Coordinating Archivist, *John Rylands University Library of Manchester*

Jennifer Holland. Assistant Director, Quality and Support, *Norfolk Library and Information Service*

Bob Oldroyd. Deputy Librarian, *Nottingham University*

Marion Shields. Executive Assistant, Pilkington Library, *Loughborough University*

Appendix E. Organisations sent letters requesting information

Commercial organisations dealing with computer disaster recovery, risk assessment and contingency planning

A1+Keyline/Computer Breakdown Insurance

AT&T Istel

ATM

Bain Hogg Risk Services

Barkers International Communications

BLCMP Library Services

Bull Information Systems

Burnett & Associates

Citidata Storage Services

Citymax Integrated Information Systems

Compact 3000

Computer Disaster Recovery

Computer Stand-By

Consultancy Corporation

Data General

Disaster Survival

Gatton Consulting Group - Synthesis Division

GEC Computer Services

Guardian Computer Services

Hewlett-Packard

Hoskyns Group , Information Security Division

IBM Business Recovery Service

Interchange Group

Olivetti UK

PCL Computer Management Services

Price Waterhouse, Information Systems Risk Management Group

Rockall Data Services

Safetynet

Syntax Managed Services

Text Systems

Unisys

Fire Services

Leicestershire Fire and Rescue Services

Government Departments/Agencies

Department of the Environment

Department of the Environment (NI)

Health and Safety Executive

Home Office, Fire Safety Division

Scottish Office

Heritage Organisations

Department of National Heritage

English Heritage

Heritage Coordination Group

Museums and Galleries Commission

National Trust

National Trust for Scotland

Royal Commission on the Historical Monuments of England

Society for the Protection of Ancient Buildings

Libraries in commercial organisations

Norton Rose (Solicitors)

Rea Brothers Limited (Merchant Bankers)

Swiss Bank Corporation

Museums

Museum of the Moving Image

National Museum of Photography, Film and Television

Overseas organisations

Association of Research Libraries, USA

Canadian Museum of Nature, Collections Division

COMLA, Jamaica (Norma Amenu-Kpodo)

Commission on Preservation and Access, USA

IFLA, PAC International Centre, France (Marie-Therese Varlamoff)

National Library of Australia, National Preservation Office

National Library of Canada (Jan Michaels)

Research Libraries Group Inc., USA

Professional bodies and trade asssociations

Association of British Insurers

Association of Conservation Officers

Association of Local Authority Risk Managers

British Automatic Sprinkler Association

British Fire Protection Systems

British Fire Services Association

British Computer Society

City Information Group

Fire Extinguishing Trades Association

Fire Protection Association

Institute of Risk Management

Library Association (Audio-Visual Group)

Library Association (Scientific Archivists Group)

Loss Prevention Council

Museum Training Institute

Records Management Society

Royal Institute of British Architects

Society of Archivists (Preservation and Conservation Group)

Salvage and recovery companies

Archival Aids

Centre for Photographic Conservation

Disaster Call

Soho Images Laboratory

Appendix F. List of Advisory Group members

The following is a list of the members of the Advisory Group who offered advice and guidance to the project team throughout the course of the project:

Professor John Feather, Dean, School of Education and Humanities, *Loughborough University*

Valerie Ferris, (then) National Preservation Officer, *National Preservation Office, British Library*

Dr Helen Forde, Head of Preservation, *Public Record Office*

Hilary Hammond, County Librarian, *Norfolk County Library and Information Service*

Chris Hunt, Director and University Librarian, *The John Rylands University of Manchester Library*

Stephanie Kenna, Research Analyst, *British Library Research and Development Department*

John McIntyre, Director of Preservation, *National Library of Scotland*

Margaret Saunders, Group Librarian, *Commercial Union Asset Management Ltd*

Appendix G. Conferences, seminars and meetings attended by the project team

Library Association, University, College and Research Group, East Midlands Section. Seminar. *Crisis and drama? Disaster planning and management in the 1990s.* Welford Place, Leicester, 28 February 1996.
Devising a disaster control plan - why and how: suggestions and guidance, paper presented by Graham Matthews.

EMALINK, Seminar. *Disaster management.* Leicester University Library, 29 November 1995.

South Wiltshire Fire Liaison Group. Symposium 3/95. *Document Protection and Recovery.* The Bibury Suite, Salisbury Racecourse, 26 September 1995.
Disaster management planning for libraries and similar premises, paper presented by Paul Eden.

State Library of New South Wales. *Redefining disasters a decade of counter-disaster planning.* Conference. Preservation Access, State Library of New South Wales, Sydney, 20-22 September, 1995.
Disaster management: guidelines for library managers, paper presented by Graham Matthews.

Library Association, North Western Branch. Seminar. *Rises from the ashes.* Lancashire County Fire Service Headquarters and Training Centre, Chorley, 24 May 1995.
Disaster control management, paper presented by Graham Matthews.

Fire Protection Association in association with English Heritage and the Isle of Wight Fire and Rescue Service. *Heritage protection '95: managing the risks.* Conference. Yarmouth, Isle of Wight, 10-12 May 1995.
Training and disaster management, paper presented by Graham Matthews.

Appendix H. Emergency equipment and supplies: suggestions for consideration

The following list of emergency equipment and supplies is based on advice from librarians, archivists, salvage and restoration experts, conservators and others with disaster experience interviewed during the project; similar lists contained in the written disaster control plans we were sent; analysis of the professional literature. It is by no means suggested, however, that all libraries will need to obtain all of the equipment and supplies listed. Selection will depend upon factors such as the size of the library, the nature of its collections and whether or not some items are already held centrally within the parent organisation (libraries should always check to see what is held centrally). Nor, for similar reasons, is it possible to say how many of each item will be needed. Bearing these factors in mind, libraries should consider keeping an appropriate selection and number of the following emergency equipment and supplies (in storage or on disaster trolleys, as applicable):

written disaster control plan

disaster trolley/wheelie bin

absorbent cloth

acid-free wrapping paper

aluminium foil

aprons (cloth)

aprons (plastic, disposable)

back supports

black bin-liners

blotting paper

boiler suits (in appropriate sizes for Disaster Response Team(s))

brushes ('yard', hard and soft)

bubblewrap

buckets (plastic)

buckets (square)

buckets with lids (plastic)

buckets with mop wringers (plastic)

bulldog clips

cassette tape recorder or 'dictaphone' (with batteries and tapes)

chalk

claw hammer

Clingfilm

clipboards and paper (lined, plain and scrap)

clothes pegs

copies of forms for recording items sent for treatment or temporary storage

copies of report forms

crates (cardboard, foldable)

crates (plastic)

crepe bandages

de-humidifiers

dust masks

dustpans and brushes

electrical extension leads

fan heaters

fans (electric, cold air)

first aid kit

floor cloths

folding 'wallpaper' tables

freezer labels (self-adhesive)

gloves (cotton, various sizes)

gloves (industrial, various sizes)

gloves (polythene, single size)

gloves (rubber, lightweight and heavy duty, various sizes)

gloves (surgical, single size)

goggles

hacksaw (with blades)

hard hats

hazard cones

hazard signs

hazard tape (black and yellow)

highlighter pens

j-cloths

labels (sticky, white waterproof)

ladder

lamps (fluorescent, with batteries)

'Melinex' sheets

mobile telephones (with batteries and charger)

mops (ordinary and 'Squeegee')

'Mylar' sheets

newsprint

notepads (waterproof and spiral)

nylon string

paintbrushes (small and medium sizes)

paper clips (brass)

paper 'kitchen' towels

pencils (HB, with sharpeners)

pencils (chinagraph)

pens (ballpoint)

pens (waterproof, marking)

pliers

polythene bags (self-sealing, assorted sizes)

polythene 'freezer' bags with ties (assorted sizes)

polythene rolls

polythene sheets

respirators (dust and mist)

rubber bands

rubber boots (appropriate sizes for Disaster Response Team(s))

sacks (heavy duty plastic)

safety pins

scissors

screwdrivers ('Phillips' and standard, in various sizes)

'Sellotape' (with dispenser)

shovel

sponges

'Stanley' knife (with blades)

stapler (with staples)

stockingette

'Swarfega'

'Sylglas' sealing tape (for leaking pipes)

tabards (fluorescent)

tape (brown parcel, with dispenser)

tape (cotton)

tape (linen)

tape (masking, with dispenser)

tape (waterproof packing, with dispenser)

tape measure

tarpaulin

torches (safety and 'head', with batteries)

vacuum cleaners (wet and dry)

washing-up liquid

waterproof coats and trousers (appropriate sizes for Disaster Response Team(s))

water pumps (electrical, submersible and non-submersible)

water pumps (hand-operated)

water spray bottles

WD40

Part two
Disaster management:
guidelines for library managers

1. Introduction

These guidelines are based on good practice highlighted during our research and should, therefore, be read in conjunction with Part One. They provide practical advice and suggestions on disaster management for library and information service managers. In particular, they are aimed at those who are about to address the issue, are in the early planning stages or are reviewing existing practices.

It is essential, however, that librarians take a proactive approach to disaster management, designing their own plans which meet their particular circumstances and requirements. The guidelines, therefore, are neither a checklist of 'things to do' or an off-the-shelf disaster control plan for use during and/or following a disaster. Rather, they focus on key points and activities, with brief notes and illustrative examples. Sources of further information and guidance are given in the bibliography at the end of the guidelines and these should be consulted for additional and more in-depth information as required.

Disaster management must address the particular circumstances of individual libraries. The type and size of library, building design and facilities, staffing levels, nature of holdings, level of automation and range of services are all crucial factors. A public branch library will have different priorities and requirements from a large research library. At the same time, all libraries will need to consider the same basic managerial issues such as risk assessment, developing staff training and finance. This is reflected in the broad-based approach which the guidelines take.

It is not intended to suggest that all actions will be necessary or appropriate for all types and size of library. Similarly, the level of reaction to any disaster and the actions taken during the reaction and recovery stages will depend on the scale of the incident. Some of the actions will already be carried out as part of other procedures such as health and safety checks, and, managers should ensure that their disaster management activities fit in with any existing or proposed organisational planning.

Any disaster, even a minor one, will cost staff time and money, cause other work to be delayed and possibly inconvenience users. Good disaster management, whilst it can never totally prevent disasters occurring, will reduce their likelihood and enable the library to deal more efficiently and effectively with them.

1.1 Arrangement of guidelines

The guidelines are arranged under four main headings:

- Prevention
- Preparedness
- Reaction
- Recovery.

Under these four main headings the following subheadings may be used:

- Advice, expertise and services
- Buildings, contents and facilities
- Collections
- Communication
- Computers
- Emergency equipment and supplies
- Finance
- Handling and salvaging damaged materials
- Health and Safety
- Human resources
- Insurance
- Public relations
- Security
- Service continuity and access
- Training
- Written disaster control plan.

Not all subheadings are included under each main heading. (For example, Service continuity and access is not included under Prevention.)

Throughout the guidelines key actions, issues and major points for consideration are highlighted in boxes. Additional comments and suggestions are given as 'bullet points' alongside.

Cross-references (where appropriate) are included at the end of each sub-section.

Prevention

2. Prevention

Prevention is better than cure!
Prevention focuses on the identification of risks to
people, collections, buildings, contents and facilities, and
the subsequent actions needed to reduce these risks,
thereby lessening the likelihood of a disaster occurring.
It is a key and vital first step in disaster management

Identify personnel with relevant expertise within the library and its parent organisation who can help with assessments of risks to people, collections, building(s), contents and facilities

- particularly useful sources of advice and expertise include:
    archivists
    buildings and estates officers
    computer specialists
    conservators
    finance officers
    health and safety officers
    insurance officers
    security personnel
- make full use of any relevant knowledge gained by experienced library staff. For example, they may have valuable information on past disasters such as why they occurred and how they were dealt with

Identify sources of advice and expertise in other libraries and archives who are willing to help with risk assessments to people, collections, building(s), contents and facilities

- particularly useful sources of advice and expertise include librarians, archivists and conservators who have carried out their own risk assessments

Identify and select commercial sources of advice, expertise and services who may be contacted to advise on or carry out risk assessments

- ask for recommendations from librarians, archivists and conservators who have used commercial sources of advice, expertise or services
- always approach individuals or companies personally and fully explain the library's needs and requirements
- particularly useful sources include:
    building surveyors
    binders
    insurers
    loss adjusters
    salvage and restoration companies
    security alarm companies

The library's local police and emergency services will also be important sources of advice and expertise

- local Fire Safety Officers and Crime Prevention Officers, for example, are particularly useful and helpful

Prevention

The Librarian or his or her deputy will need to tour the inside and outside of the library with buildings experts to carry out assessments of risk to building(s), contents and facilities

- suitable expertise may be available within the parent organisation, for example, in buildings and estates or health and safety departments, or identified and brought in on a consultancy basis
- be sure to consider preventive maintenance measures including redecoration
- identify and assess risks according to their probability and likely impact on core services
- decide what needs to be done as soon as possible, what needs to be done, and, therefore, budgeted for, at a later date and what can be given a low priority
- cost (get at least three quotes) and make a strong case for any building work, repairs or new systems
- draw up a prioritised work programme based on risk assessments and costings

---

Check building maintenance records to determine whether or not any underlying defects are manifesting themselves as recurrent faults

- underlying defects in electrical, water, sewerage and drainage systems often manifest themselves as recurrent faults

---

Arrange for building(s), contents and facilities to be regularly inspected (at least annually)

- establish maintenance records and ensure that they are kept fully up to date
- report and record any problems immediately, and instigate formal procedures for following up any actions or repairs that need to be taken

---

Ensure that staff are aware of who is responsible for buildings, contents and facilities including any necessary remedial work

- ensure that staff are aware of formal procedures for reporting faults and any other problems

---

Continues...

Keep a defect book

- keeping a defect book enables relatively minor recurring problems to be spotted more easily before they become serious. For example, several small floods following fairly heavy downpours may become a library under two feet of water following a weekend of storms if the drains causing the problem are not properly dealt with!
- ensure staff report any problems with building(s), contents or facilities immediately
- record:
    - the date and who reported the problem
    - the nature of the problem
    - the person responsible for ensuring that the problem is brought to the attention of senior library managers and appropriate organisational departments such as buildings and estates
    - any subsequent actions taken
- the Disaster Manager should inspect and sign the defect book each month

Contact the local fire service and ask the Fire Safety Officer to carry out a fire safety inspection of the library

- section 1(i)(f) of the Fire Services Act 1947 places a duty on fire authorities to give advice, when requested, "in respect of buildings and other property in the area of the fire authority as to fire prevention, restricting the spread of fires, and means of escape in case of fire"
- the library may require a fire certificate under the Fire Precautions Act 1971. If it does not already have one, it will need to find out from its local fire service whether or not one is required

Be aware that fire safety legislation is concerned with protecting and saving human life, and not with protecting buildings and contents *per se*

- fire authorities will advise on protecting stock if asked, but be specific about which items, collections or areas of the library (for example, special collections rooms or other areas not in heavy use or occupied) need to be protected and the degree of protection required

Continues...

Install smoke detectors and consider installing smoke extractors and/or sprinklers, particularly in areas where valuable or irreplaceable items or collections are stored

Ensure that all fire-extinguishers and any automatic safety systems such as fire-alarms, smoke detectors, smoke extractors and sprinklers are tested regularly and maintained by qualified inspectors

- take advice on the selection of fire extinguishers
- the correct types of fire extinguisher must be kept in appropriate locations throughout the library, and be properly maintained by an internal fire safety officer or a reputable servicing company
- ensure that any smoke detectors and sprinkler heads are kept clear of obstructions
- install an automatic system for switching off air-conditioning in the event of a fire
- do not forget basements!

Pay special attention to potential fire hazards such as faulty electrical wiring, overloaded power points, electrical equipment including kettles in staff rooms, computers and photocopiers, combustible refuse and inflammable substances

Keep fire-doors closed at all times

- check that a sufficient number of fire doors are correctly installed with the local fire authority's Fire Safety Officer (in larger organisations this may be the responsibility of a health and safety/fire officer)
- fire doors should either be self-closing or be closed automatically by an activated alarm
- check that fire-doors are closed as part of daily locking-up routines

Continues...

Prevention

Ensure that the integrity of fire-walls and doors is not compromised by any refurbishment or building work	• take advice on building more fire-walls to increase compartmentation of open-plan or large storage areas

Pay special attention to potential water damage from leaking roofs, guttering, windows, radiators and water, sewerage and drainage systems	• consider installing water detectors, barriers, sumps or additional drainage systems in areas prone to flooding, particularly in basement storage areas • if possible, remove or drain any water tanks, and redirect water pipes, above or next to collections and computer rooms (pay particular attention to spaces created by artificial floors and ceilings) • consider installing drainage points in floors (floors will need to be waterproofed if this is done) • consider building sumps into basement floors to facilitate the use of pumps • the local fire service's Fire Safety Officer will usually give verbal advice regarding any particular flooding problems during fire safety inspections

Establish good working practices for outside contractors working in and around the library, and monitor contractors to ensure that these practices are followed	• draw up and implement a policy on working practices for outside contractors. Require outside contractors to comply with these practices • restrict access into the building for outside contractors by means of an entry control system • pay particular attention to fire risks associated with the use of welding equipment, blow-torches and electrical appliances. Prohibit the use of welding equipment and blow torches in areas where valuable items and collections are stored • issue permits to outside contractors carrying out 'hot work'. This permit should require them to keep appropriate fire extinguishers to hand wherever the work is being carried out • ensure that stock is properly protected during building work (for example, cover with plastic sheeting or move to temporary storage)

Continues...

Prevention

Separate storage areas from work areas and use them solely for this purpose

- allow only authorised personnel in storage areas
- do not keep photocopiers or any other unnecessary electrical equipment in storage areas

Establish good housekeeping practices and routines throughout the library and its environs

- ensure that:
    all areas in and around the library are kept free from accumulated refuse such as packing
    waste paper is stacked in a safe, secure place to await collection
    gangways between stacks and shelving are kept clear at all times
    drains are kept clear of leaves and other debris
    shelves and library stock are dusted regularly (and carefully, so as not to cause damage)
    cupboards, lift shafts, ceiling spaces and similar areas are kept free from dust and rubbish
    cleaners regularly dust and keep clean pipes, radiators, ducting and electrical fittings
    mobile shelving is kept in good working order
- encourage staff to keep their own working areas tidy, and consider whether or not a 'clear desk' policy is appropriate in certain areas of the library

Ensure that environmental conditions will not be adversely affected before carrying out any refurbishment or rebuilding work

- The National Preservation Office recommends the following conditions (NPO, 1992):

    temperature (degrees C):
paper and parchment	13-18
magnetic media	4-16
sound recordings	10-21
microfilm and photographic materials	below 20

    relative humidity (%):
paper and parchment	55-65
magnetic media	40-55
sound recordings	40-60
microfilm and photographic materials	30-40

Continues...

80

Prevention

If in any doubt, always get expert advice!

- buildings experts should be identified as part of disaster prevention activities

See also:
Prevention. Advice, expertise and services
Prevention. Finance
Prevention. Health and safety
Prevention. Security

Ensure that risks to collections are understood and taken into consideration by those carrying out building risk assessments	• identify and assess risks according to their probability and likely resulting damage to collections • make a strong case for any necessary improvements (for example, better shelving and storage conditions) • if commissioning risk assessments, be specific about which items or collections need to be protected and the degree of protection required

Pay special attention to fire hazards, water ingress, environmental conditions and security	• keep stock away from hot water pipes and electric light fittings • identify and safely isolate fire hazards such as nitrate film • monitor environmental conditions, especially temperature and relative humidity, in areas where valuable items and collections are kept

When designing the layout of collections, take account of how the most important or valuable items and collections can be best protected environmentally and in terms of security	• keep all items off floors and valuable items off lower shelves • do not site collections above or next to any water tanks or pipes • consider installing trays under water pipes or joints, with outlet pipes to channel any leaks away to external gutters or drains • consider installing protective canopies over shelving • have separate electrical circuits in special collections rooms and isolate when the rooms are not in use • avoid storing stock on the floor

Inspect collections regularly (at least annually)	• report and record any problems immediately, and instigate formal procedures for prioritising and carrying out any necessary conservation • ask staff (including cleaners) to look out for and report any early signs of damage to individual items

Shelve books neatly and compactly	• a 'solid block' of books will not burn as readily as a loose array

Continues...

Prevention

Box archive collections

- boxing will protect collections from dust, reduce smoke damage and reduce the risk of water damage from fire hoses or sprinklers
- use 'acid-free' preservation quality boxes

If in any doubt, always get expert advice!

- archivists and conservators should be identified and approached as part of disaster prevention activities

83

Encourage staff to be vigilant at all times regarding the safety and security of people, buildings, contents, facilities and collections, and to report and record any problems they come across immediately

- ensure that staff know the names and contact details of any fire marshals and health and safety officers
- ensure that staff are aware of the correct reporting and recording procedures
- ensure staff are aware of who is responsible for buildings, contents, facilities and collections
- stress the need for staff to be particularly vigilant during refurbishment or building work, especially when outside contractors are working in the library

In a shared building, establish working hours and out of working hours contact procedures with other occupant(s) to ensure that the library is informed of any incidents which occur elsewhere in the building and which might affect the library's collections, contents or facilities

- identify and establish a good working relationship with those responsible for building maintenance and security
- maintain good relations with any other occupant(s) - there may be scope for mutually beneficial activities and arrangements

See also:
Prevention. Public relations

| Instigate regular, systematic backup procedures for computer systems, PCs, files and commercial and custom software | • ensure that staff working with computers are aware of systematic backup procedures, and that these are followed
• establish system security, backup procedures and recovery requirements with computing service providers |

| Base the frequency of backup, the number of copies made and how and where they should be stored on an assessment of the impact of data loss on the library's services | • keep crucial data backups such as system software in secure fireproof environments, preferably off-site (for example, with a commercial storage agency)
• ensure that the often essential software and files held by secretarial and administrative staff on their own PCs are backed up. Floppy disk copies of these files should be kept in a separate location, preferably off-site
• consider system hard-disk backup options such as disk-mirroring or RAID (Redundant Array of Independent Disks)
• always keep floppy disks on desks in closed disk boxes for extra protection (for example, from the effects of smoke during a fire)
• consider carrying out a risk assessment and review annually |

| Periodically check all backup tapes and disks to ensure the integrity of data on them | • keep all magnetic data storage media away from magnetic fields, heat, smoke, dust and high humidity levels |

| Periodically check to ensure that computer systems can in fact be restored with backup copies of software and data | |

Continues...

Prevention

Make arrangements with system suppliers for them to provide emergency support in the event of a system failure

- these may be included in maintenance contracts

Staff must be properly trained in the use of new software, including upgrades, to reduce the risk of accidental loss or corruption of existing data

- identify priority staff and priority software

Establish a written policy and formal procedures to combat viruses

- procedures should include:
    the use of anti-virus software
    booting from hard-disk by default
    a ban on staff and users loading their own software onto the library's computers
    regular audits of hard and floppy disks
    scanning portable PCs, including those of authorised users, before connecting them to networks
- use passwords for networked systems and change them regularly

Isolate computers on separate electrical circuits.

- consider fitting surge-suppression equipment to these circuits
- consider using UPS (Uninterruptible Power Supply) to ensure stable power supply during voltage fluctuations, and to ensure short term power supply (for example, 15-30 minutes) during power cuts to enable a managed shutdown of systems

Keep master copies of all manuals safe and secure from theft and sign out copies if borrowed

Continues...

86

Establish a no drinking, eating or
smoking policy in computer rooms and
for all staff using computers

If in any doubt, always get expert advice!

- service providers and other computer specialists will have
been identified as part of disaster prevention activities

See also:
Prevention. Training

Finance will need to be made available to carry out risk assessments to people, building(s), contents, facilities and collections

- remember that there is likely to be a charge even if risk assessments are carried out by other departments in the parent organisation
- insurers may carry out risk assessments without charge

Obtain at least three estimates for any necessary building work,
repairs or new systems and present a prioritised list of these to the finance committee or department as appropriate

See also:
Prevention. Buildings, contents and facilities

Prevention

Establish a policy and procedures for switching off electrical equipment when not in use and as part of 'end of day' routines

Designate all areas where stock is kept as nonsmoking areas and strictly enforce no smoking in these areas

- establish a policy on smoking (that is, designate areas where smoking is permitted)

Provide noncombustible containers, in addition to ordinary waste-containers, for cigarette ends in areas where smoking is permitted

- ensure that noncombustible containers are emptied daily
- remember to provide noncombustible containers at entrances to the library if staff and users smoke outside

Keep storage of inflammable liquids to a minimum. Store separately and safely in secure containers in appropriate environmental conditions, preferably away from other buildings

- ensure that only the minimum amount of inflammable liquid is taken into the library to do the job at hand
- ensure that containers are returned to safe storage immediately after use
- ensure safe disposal of empty containers

Keep storage of gas cylinders to a minimum. Store separately and safely in appropriate environmental conditions, preferably away from other buildings

- ensure that gas cylinders are taken into the library only when required
- ensure safe disposal of empty cylinders
- ensure that outside contractors follow the same practices as staff when using gas cylinders

Continues...

Restrict the use of portable heaters.
Ensure that any that are used are stable
and are kept well away from
combustible materials

- do not place anything on top of any heaters, portable or otherwise

Note:

Compliance with Health and Safety legislation will, of course, be necessary. All staff must be aware of their statutory responsibilities regarding their own and other people's health and safety. Library managers should read, and have available for reference, relevant health and safety guidelines such as those published by the Health and Safety Executive. (See Bibliography.)

See also:
Prevention. Buildings, contents and facilities
Prevention. Training

Prevention

Encourage the public to be vigilant and to report anything suspicious to library staff during working hours or to the police outside working hours

- post notices in the library highlighting any particular problems or occurrences that the public might be able to help with

See also:
Prevention. Communication

Prevention

A well-maintained library with visible signs of good security practices and alert, security-conscious staff will discourage theft, vandalism and other criminal activity

- always maintain a suitable level of lighting outside working hours to deter break-ins
- test all alarm systems regularly (at least once a week)

Make a senior member of the library staff responsible for security

- the person responsible for security will:
  ensure that the library's security policy is fully integrated with its policy on building maintenance, health and safety and training
  be responsible for liaison with organisational security personnel and the police
  report to the Disaster Manager

Advice can be obtained from the local police forces's Crime Prevention Officer, security consultants, commercial security services or security equipment suppliers

- only seek advice from consultants and commercial companies known to be reputable to the Crime Prevention Officer
- burglar alarm suppliers should be members of the British Security Industry Association (BSIA) or the National Approval Council for Security Systems (NACOSS)

Carry out building security risk assessments

- pay particular attention to:
  doors and door frames
  window frames and glass
  skylights

'Design out' crime

- try to ensure that the layout of the library allows any user to be seen by at least one member of staff, and that there are no 'blind spots'

Continues...

92

Install high quality locks and ensure that doors, windows and skylights fit properly in their frames	• there may be some conflict between optimising security and ensuring the safe evacuation of the building in the event of a fire. If in doubt, always check with the local fire service's Fire Safety Officer
Carry out collections and contents security risk assessments	• pay particular attention to valuable and/or sought after items and collections such as archives, computers, compact discs and videos • decide which items are most likely to be targeted by thieves or vandals and afford them greater protection • remember that information is a 'commodity', and that data theft may be a serious risk for some libraries
Alarm emergency fire exits not in normal use	
Consider installing electronic alarm systems or Closed-Circuit Television (CCTV) to protect vulnerable areas of the building and particularly valuable or high risk items	• only use companies known to be reputable to the local police force's Crime Prevention Officer • get at least three quotes for any work to be done • balance costs against risks and do not buy on price alone
Establish step-by-step locking up procedures throughout the library and its environs. Ensure that the last staff to leave the building are fully aware of locking up procedures, and that these are always followed	• keys should be kept in a lockable case, in a location accessible only to library staff

Continues...

Prevention

Restrict access to storage areas to
authorised personnel

Use metal containers for book drops
and place in areas away from
inflammable materials

Bomb threats must always be taken
seriously, and staff should always be on
the look out for any suspicious looking
packages

- establish bomb threat procedures
- designate safety areas to which staff and readers can be moved
- consider installing toughened glass in windows or covering existing windows with security film

Always remember that effective
security depends as much upon the
loyalty, goodwill and vigilance of staff
as it does upon good locks and security
systems

- ensure that staff are aware of the need for vigilance at all times regarding the security of buildings, collections and contents, and for anything suspicious to be reported immediately

See also:
Prevention. Buildings, contents and facilities
Prevention. Training

Prevention

Include disaster prevention awareness-raising on induction courses for all new staff, and provide regular 'refresher' courses for existing staff

- ensure that all staff are aware of risks to people, collections, building(s), contents and facilities
- ensure that all staff are aware that any problems should be reported immediately
- ensure that all staff know to whom they should report any problems
- ensure that all staff are aware of nonsmoking areas

Ensure that staff using computers are aware of backup procedures and other disaster prevention measures

Stress the need for staff to be especially vigilant during refurbishment or other building work

Encourage staff to develop a 'health and safety consciousness', rather than simply be aware of their statutory requirements

- people's health and safety must be the primary concern of disaster management

See also:
Prevention. Computers
Prevention. Health and safety
Prevention. Security

95

Preparedness

3. Preparedness

Being prepared should enable the library to respond more
quickly and more effectively to disasters, thereby
reducing their effects and facilitating recovery

Preparedness

| Sources of advice, expertise and services must be identified and included in written disaster control plans | |

| Identify relevant expertise within the library and its parent organisation and maximise the use of this expertise throughout the library's disaster planning activities | • particularly useful sources of advice and expertise include:
    archivists
    buildings and estates officers
    conservators
    finance officers
    health and safety officers
    insurance officers |

| Identify sources of advice and expertise in other libraries and archives who are willing to offer advice on drawing up disaster control plans or to provide assistance in the event of a disaster | • particularly useful sources of advice and expertise include:
    librarians and archivists who have written their own disaster control plans
    librarians and archivists with disaster experience |

| Join or consider establishing a local and/or regional network of mutual support with other libraries and archives | • possible benefits include:
    access to conservation expertise and advice
    central storage of emergency equipment and supplies
    cost-sharing
    joint training activities
    temporary accommodation and storage facilities
• other institutions such as museums or galleries may be willing to participate |

| Contact the local fire service and ask the Fire Safety Officer to advise on fire safety | • fire services visit the more complex buildings in their areas as part of general familiarisation programmes
• some fire services *may* keep floor plans of libraries showing collections prioritised for salvage in 'action portfolios' at local stations |

Continues...

Identify and select commercial sources of advice, expertise and services who can be contacted in the event of a disaster	• always approach individuals or companies personally and fully explain the library's needs and requirements • ask individuals or companies what services they offer and what they cost. Some companies have membership schemes which offer lower rates for services and/or priority response • ask individuals or companies for contacts in other libraries or archives who have used their services • ensure that '24hr emergency service' does not mean that an answerphone is switched on outside normal office hours!

The following sources of advice, expertise and services will need to be considered:

archival storage and equipment suppliers
audiovisual materials salvage and restoration services
binders
builders
carpenters
computer software and hardware suppliers
computer data storage facilities
computer software salvage and restoration services
computer hardware salvage and restoration services
conservators
decorators
deepfreeze storage facilities
disaster recovery service providers
electricians
electricity suppliers
emergency equipment suppliers
 (for example, cold air fans, dehumidifiers)
emergency boarding contractors

environmental specialists
freeze and vacuum-drying facilities
gas suppliers
glaziers
industrial cleaners
insurers
locksmiths
paper salvage and restoration services
photographic materials restoration services
plasterers
plastic crate suppliers
plumbers
prefabricated temporary building suppliers
roofing contractors
security alarm companies
shelving and storage equipment suppliers
temporary storage facilities
transportation and removal companies

Check local directories and ask other librarians and archivists to recommend any local and/or national services they may have used	• The National Preservation Office, based at the British Library, may also be able to suggest contacts • published written disaster control plans, guides and directories include details of services, and these may be used as a starting point. Each library, however, must decide which individuals or companies to approach for up to date information in order to determine their suitability

Preparedness

The correct types of fire extinguisher must be kept in appropriate locations throughout the library, and be properly maintained by a reputable servicing company	• in a larger organisation this may be the responsibility of a fire safety officer. The library, however, should still check equipment to ensure that servicing is carried out at regular intervals • if in any doubt regarding any fire safety equipment, contact the local fire service's fire safety officer • site both CO_2 and water extinguishers at each fire point within collection areas
Obtain or compile floor plans showing electrical, gas, heating, water, sewerage, drainage and air-conditioning systems	• highlight stopcocks, isolation valves and fire-risers • include these floor plans in the written disaster control plan
Produce a series of floor plans showing evacuation routes, emergency exits, assembly points and the location of fire extinguishers and fire-risers	• display these floor plans in prominent locations throughout the library • include these floor plans in the written disaster control plan

Prioritise individual items and collections for salvage on a methodical basis, and with reference to different disaster scenarios. Include floor plans showing these prioritised items and collections in the library's written disaster control plan

- prioritisation will depend upon the following criteria:
  - how easily items or collections could be replaced, and at what cost
  - impact of loss on the library's core services
  - monetary value
  - vulnerability
  - whether or not items or collections are unique or replaceable
- prioritised floor plans will be extremely useful for fire officers should they have an opportunity - and be willing to - salvage any items during and immediately after a fire

Consider redesigning the layout of the library, taking account of how quickly and easily the most important or valuable items and collections could be removed if they are damaged or at risk following a disaster

- take care not to compromise the security of any items or collections
- consider alternative routes and exits for removing items from the library; identify features such as stairways and ramps which may be difficult to negotiate with heavy books or trolleys

Record details of storage requirements for collections in case any need to be moved into temporary storage following a disaster

- record:
  - floor loadings
  - shelving strengths
  - shelving capacity
- remember that stock kept on mobile shelving will require a lot more space if temporarily housed on fixed shelving

Keep up to date copies of catalogues at a separate location in a secure, fireproof environment, preferably off-site

- up to date copies of catalogues (for example, microfiche security copies of manual catalogues) will be invaluable when replacing lost or damaged stock, or when making an insurance claim

Continues...

Keep photographic or video records of significant individual items or collections

- proof of loss will be required when making an insurance claim. Should catalogues be destroyed, photographic or video records may assist compilation of stock lists

Proper documentation of collections, including clear, permanent, waterproof labelling of boxed collections will assist in the control and identification of stock during reaction and recovery

Keep master negatives of any microfilms of the library's own stock of rare materials made for preservation purposes in secure, fireproof environments, preferably off-site

Instructions on handling and salvaging different types of material should be prepared for use during a disaster response

Continues...

Compile a checklist of possible handling, salvage and conservation methods for the different materials held in the collections

- discuss options with conservation experts, to determine methods of handling, salvage and conservation likely to be used during reaction and recovery
- include guidance on handling, salvage and conservation methods in the written disaster control plan
- include practical handling and salvage sessions in training courses

See also:
Preparedness. Handling and salvaging damaged materials

Preparedness

Keep brief, easy to follow instructions for raising the alarm and lists of personnel to be contacted in the event of a disaster next to all telephones

- list names in the order in which they should be contacted, for example, the Disaster Reaction Manager(s) first
- include office telephone numbers, job titles and the departments or sections in which each Disaster Response Team member works
- for Disaster Response Team members to be contacted outside normal working hours include home telephone numbers, addresses and whether or not they have their own transport
- ensure that Disaster Response Team members keep copies of lists at home so that they can telephone other members as necessary
- ensure that security staff - including any in organisational security lodges or external security companies with responsibility for library security - have copies of instructions and lists
- ensure that any staff working outside 'normal' working hours such as cleaners have copies of instructions and lists. Disasters often occur when libraries are closed and these staff may easily be the first to discover an incident

Names, telephone numbers and addresses of keyholders should be given to the local police force

- ensure that this does not conflict with any organisational security policy regarding direct contact with the emergency services
- these details may also be needed by others who might have cause to call out keyholders such as external security companies

Keep all contact lists fully up to date and ensure that staff on contact lists leave alternative telephone numbers where they can be contacted should they be away from the library on business

- do not forget to delete details of staff who retire or leave, or to add new staff as necessary
- do not forget to include lists held by the local police force!
- check the accuracy of lists at least annually

Continues...

It may not be feasible or considered necessary to have a member of the Disaster Response Team on permanent stand-by outside normal working hours. If so, an appropriate number of the Disaster Response Team should be contactable outside normal working hours

- an 'appropriate number' will depend on the availability of staff. It is recommended that, if possible, at least three members of the Disaster Response Team are contactable outside normal working hours
- identify any 24hr emergency contacts or services within the library's parent organisation. Include details of these in the disaster control plan

Mobile telephones are extremely useful for maintaining communications if land-lines have been lost, or when investigating and dealing with problems in large buildings

- consider including mobile telephones in stocks of emergency equipment
- test different types of mobile telephone at various locations throughout the library in order to identify any potential problems before buying
- check battery charging times
- keep an adequate supply of spare batteries and test regularly

In a shared building, establish working hours and out of working hours contact procedures with other occupant(s) to ensure that each is immediately informed of any incident

See also:
Preparedness. Human resources
Preparedness. Public relations
Preparedness. Service continuity and access

Preparedness

Instigate emergency backup procedures for staff using computers to follow in the event of a disaster

Designated staff may need to know how to shut down computer systems, or, alternatively, know when to inform service providers to do so, according to predetermined circumstances

Compile documentation to enable faults to be reported and computer systems restored in the absence of the computer manager or other senior computing staff

- wherever possible, keep documentation simple and easy to understand so that, if necessary, staff can give details to, and take instructions from, those trying to restore systems
- documentation should be kept in a 'disaster box' along with consumables and a selection of cables and leads, preferably off-site
- documentation should include:
    system operating instructions and procedures
    anti-virus procedures
    passwords and access levels
    network configurations (including external network diagrams, LANS and physical layout of cabling, patch panels, power systems and power points)
    setup parameters
    inventories of operating manuals, hardware (including manufacturer, model and serial numbers) and software (including version)
    names, addresses and telephone numbers of suppliers
    copies of insurance policies, warranties and service agreements

See also:
Preparedness. Insurance
Preparedness. Service continuity and access
Preparedness. Training

Preparedness

Keep emergency equipment and supplies on mobile disaster trolleys or in wheelie bins ready for immediate use

- carefully consider where disaster trolleys or wheelie bins should be kept. For example, they must be easily accessible and in larger libraries placed at strategic points through the building(s)
- disaster trolleys should be light enough and small enough for two people to move easily around the building, including up and down stairs
- do not use locks on disaster trolleys or wheelie bins. Use plastic tags or sticky labels on lids or doors that will break on opening. Check these regularly to ensure that trolleys or bins have not been tampered with or contents removed
- check stocks regularly to ensure none are missing or past their 'sell-by' date
- replace any stock found missing or out of date as soon as possible

---

Keep backup stocks of emergency equipment and supplies held on disaster trolleys or in wheelie bins. Keep larger equipment for an immediate response to more serious incidents

- keep stocks locked away, but ensure that keys are readily available if needed
- make a member of the Disaster Response Team responsible for looking after the emergency equipment and supplies
- check stocks regularly to ensure none are missing or past their 'sell-by' date
- establish a routine for regularly recharging batteries in mobile telephones and testing/replacing batteries for other emergency equipment such as torches
- check emergency equipment such as generators, pumps cold air fans and dehumifiers regularly to ensure that it is in good working order
- replace any stock found missing or out of date as soon as possible
- review stocks annually to decide whether or not any new equipment or supplies should be included, and/or any existing equipment is no longer required
- ensure that there is 24hr access to any stocks kept off-site (for example, if held centrally as part of a cooperative initiative)
- 'flight bags' containing protective clothing and emergency equipment and supplies for immediate use can be kept in car boots of Disaster Response Team(s)
- savings may be made if emergency equipment and supplies are bought by bulk purchase in cooperation with other libraries or departments within the parent organisation

Continues..

Preparedness

> Ensure that all staff know that emergency equipment and supplies are available, where they are kept, who is responsible for them and where any keys are kept

Set up a disaster contingency fund in consultation with organisational finance officers	• major spending decisions will be the responsibility of the Disaster Manager, but the Disaster Reaction Manager(s) may need to make quick spending decisions based on an assessment of a disaster situation
Establish procedures for quick approval and raising of orders and processing of invoices	• be aware of the impact of a major disaster on the parent organisation's finance and administration departments. Work loads will increase considerably

Draw up instructions on handling and salvaging different types of material for use during a disaster response	• instructions on handling and salvaging damaged materials will be included in written disaster control plans
There is considerable guidance in the literature on the various methods and techniques of dealing with different kinds of damaged materials	• reading this literature this will provide useful background and an insight into appropriate actions. There is, however, no substitute for practical experience, and 'hands-on' training with damaged materials is essential • be aware that expert opinions may differ! • try to keep up to date with new techniques and emergency equipment and supplies
Take expert conservation advice on handling and salvaging damaged materials	• sources of conservation advice within the library or its parent organisation, or other libraries or archives, who are willing to give advice on handling and salvaging damaged materials, should be identified and consulted as part of disaster preparedness activities • always approach reputable individuals and companies, but bear in mind that conservators may disagree over some issues; if in any doubt, take a second or third opinion!
Disaster Response Teams must be given 'hands-on' training in handling and salvaging the different types of material in the library's collections	• consider organising cooperative training sessions with other libraries or archives on a local or regional basis • look out for training courses run by professional bodies and commercial organisations

See also:
Preparedness. Collections
Preparedness. Human resources

Preparedness

Notices outlining procedures for raising the alarm should be displayed in prominent positions throughout the library

• ensure that notices are kept unobstructed from view at all times

Notices showing evacuation routes, emergency exits and assembly points should be displayed in prominent positions throughout the library

• ensure that notices are kept unobstructed from view at all times

Test fire alarms at least once a week and carry out regular and random fire drills

Maintain clear access along evacuation routes and keep emergency exits unobstructed at all times

Adequate supplies of protective clothing and equipment must be available for Disaster Response Teams in appropriate sizes

> Appoint someone at the highest level to act as Disaster Manager with overall responsibility for disaster management

- the Disaster Manager may delegate day to day responsibility for disaster management, but will always ensure that it receives due attention at senior management level

> Appoint a member, or members, of staff to write a disaster control plan

- the person(s) drawing up the plan must:
    - be able to write clearly and concisely
    - have the ability and confidence to communicate and negotiate with senior staff from other departments within their own organisation, and with similar staff in other organisations
- if they are not senior managers themselves they must have full support at this level
- some libraries appoint a committee to draw up their written disaster control plan, while others give this responsibility to an appropriate member of staff (for example, someone who already has responsibility for buildings or health and safety). This will depend upon the organisational ethos and structure within which the library operates

> Appoint member(s) of staff to act as Disaster Reaction Manager(s) with responsibility for coordinating immediate disaster reaction and recovery, and managing Disaster Response Teams

- select Disaster Reaction Manager(s) on the basis of their personal qualities, expertise and experience rather than simply seniority. They must:
    - be good team leaders
    - be able to remain calm under pressure
    - have the confidence of other staff
- the Disaster Reaction Manager(s) must have the full support of the Disaster Manager, and be given the authority to make their own decisions, including spending decisions, during any initial disaster reaction and recovery
- unless there is 24hr security cover and access, the Disaster Reaction Manager(s) must be authorised keyholders

Continues...

<table>
<tr>
<td>

Select and train suitable staff for Disaster Response Teams

</td>
<td>

- Disaster Response Team members should be selected and organised according to:
  - an ability to work in teams
  - an ability to work under instruction, but to be able to show initiative and flexibility
  - any specialist education or training they may have received (for example in conservation or health and safety)
  - their ability to remain calm under pressure
  - their physical capabilities
- in a larger scale disaster - staffing levels permitting, separate teams will needed for protecting undamaged stock, setting up temporary storage and drying areas, sorting damaged items according to type of material, damage and proposed conservation treatment, cleaning, drying, packing and removing items for storage or treatment
- unless there is 24hr security cover and access, any Disaster Response Team Member(s) on call out lists must be authorised keyholders

</td>
</tr>
<tr>
<td>

Consider appointing someone at the highest level to act as Disaster Recovery Manager in the event of a large-scale disaster

</td>
<td>

- The Disaster Recovery Manager will be responsible for ensuring service continuity and access. S/he will need to plan for the short, medium and long term needs of the service. This will involve activities such as:
  - advising staff and users of temporary services and facilities
  - arranging temporary accommodation and storage
  - dealing with offers of help which may or may not be needed
  - ensuring staff counselling is available
  - establishing temporary service points (for example, to provide reference and loan facilities)
  - liaison with staff in other departments in the parent organisation such as finance, buildings and estates
  - liaison with the Media and Liaison Officer
  - stock replacement
- appointing a Disaster Recovery Manager will allow the Disaster Reaction Manager to concentrate on immediate reaction and recovery activities such as handling and salvaging damaged materials
- there will need to be close liaison between the Disaster Recovery Manager and the Disaster Reaction Manager

</td>
</tr>
</table>

Continues...

Preparedness

Note:

Although the roles and responsibilities of the Disaster Manager, the Disaster Reaction Manager and the Disaster Recovery Manager are described separately, they may have to be undertaken by the same person, particularly in smaller libraries

See also:
Preparedness. Communication
Preparedness. Handling and salvaging damaged materials
Preparedness. Service continuity and access
Preparedness. Training

Preparedness

Check the library's insurance policy with insurers to ascertain the types of disaster for which it is insured

- the library and its collections should at least be insured against fire, flood, storm, theft, malicious damage, riot, terrorism, explosion and aircraft
- it may be necessary to identify and negotiate with staff such as finance officers with responsibility for insurance within the parent organisation

Check the library's insurance policy with insurers to ensure adequate cover is provided

- ensure adequate cover is provided for:
    buildings (repair and rebuilding)
    collections (conservation and/or replacement)
    contents (including computers and other office equipment)
    consequential losses (that is, any increased costs and additional expenses incurred as a direct result of a disaster such as salvage operations and loss of revenue)
    fixtures and fittings
    legal liability to employees and public
    personal injury or death to employees and public

Identify any limitations contained in the library's insurance policy and consider whether or not they are acceptable (most will be standard practice)

- limitations may include:
    maximum indemnity period - the length of time following a disaster for which consequential losses are payable
    exclusions - any specific incidents which may be excluded
    time franchises - any delays in the time following a disaster before the terms of the policy come into force
    material damage proviso - states that insurance premiums are paid up at the time of the disaster, and sets any 'excess' or 'deductible', that is, the minimum level of loss below which no insurance is payable, or, alternatively, the amount which will be deducted from the payment of a larger claim
    sum insured - the maximum amount payable

Check the library's insurance policy with insurers to ascertain the position regarding cover for staff working in Disaster Response Teams

- staff may be asked to work in unfamiliar and potentially hazardous conditions during a disaster (for example, in the dark or in water). They must be covered for doing this - even during training sessions

Continues

114

Have important or valuable items and collections valued and inform insurers and finance officers of anything of particular value	• check with insurers to see whether or not separate or additional cover is required for individual items over a certain value • compare the cost of any additional insurance cover required for important or valuable items with the cost of taking preventive measures to provide additional protection • any irreplaceable items which cannot be properly valued such as archives or unique historical documents should be covered for estimated conservation costs • informing insurers of any particularly valuable items and collections should reduce the likelihood of any problems following a claim
Inform insurers as soon as the library has carried out risk assessments to buildings and collections and has written a disaster control plan as part of a coherent disaster management strategy	• although it is unlikely that premiums will be reduced, having a written disaster control plan will demonstrate good managerial practice, while risk assessments will help insurers to calculate realistic premiums. These factors should reduce the likelihood of any problems following a claim
Inform insurers of any changes in circumstances which may affect premiums or any future claims	• premiums may be reduced following the installation of any fire detection or suppression systems • future claims may be affected if insurers are unaware of the acquisition of any particularly valuable items or collections, or the purchase of any expensive equipment such as computer systems
Always remember that the insured must prove loss when making any claims	• keep up to date copies of catalogues and inventories of office furniture and equipment such as computers and photocopiers. If possible keep them in separate, fireproof environments, preferably off-site • keep photographic or video records of library buildings and individual items or collections

Continues...

Preparedness

Most computer software and hardware will be covered under existing insurance policies. The wording in some 'traditional' policies, however, may be ambiguous when applied to computer networks using custom software

- the library may need to ensure that its insurance policy meets its needs concerning:
  - all network software and hardware
  - cabling
  - data insurance
  - disasters occurring as a result of errors in writing software, operating the system or using an individual work station
  - time spent restoring corrupt data
  - the consequences of working with corrupt data
  - third party liability (for example, faulty cable installation)
- inform insurers of any new equipment purchases or upgrades immediately

See also:
Preparedness. Computers

Depending on what else is considered 'newsworthy' on the day, even a relatively minor disaster may attract media attention	• the library should try to build up a good relationship with the local media as part of its normal PR activities; the local media can be very helpful in the event of a disaster, for example, by relaying information on contingency arrangements and issuing appeals to help to replace lost collections
Appoint a senior member of staff to act as Media Liaison Officer in the event of any media interest following a disaster	• the Media Liaison Officer should establish a rapport with the parent organisation's media and public relations officers so that they are both 'on the same wavelength' should a disaster generate media interest
Following a disaster, direct all media enquiries to the Media Liaison Officer	• ensure that all staff know who the Media Liaison Officer is • ensure that all staff are aware of the need not to answer media enquiries themselves, but to direct all enquiries to the Media Liaison Officer
Prepare a list of important clients or user groups who are to be contacted immediately in the event of a serious disruption to services which will affect them	• inform users of what has happened, what is being done to restore services and when services are likely to be restored; be realistic rather than overly optimistic • taking the initiative will save considerable time dealing with incoming telephone enquiries, and allow the library to manage the situation • make contingency arrangements for emergency telephone lines

See also:
Preparedness. Communication

> Provide security staff, caretakers and cleaners with brief, easy to follow instructions for contacting designated members of the Disaster Response Team in the event of a disaster occurring outside library working hours

- ensure that any damage, or potential damage, to the library or any of its contents is reported to a member of the Disaster Response Team; damaged materials may suffer further damage if not treated quickly, or if wrongly handled (even with the best of intentions)

> The police will not normally search a building themselves following a bomb threat. Library staff may, therefore, be called upon to carry out bomb searches

- include building searches in induction courses and disaster training programmes

See also:
Preparedness. Training

Preparedness

> Make contingency arrangements for temporary accommodation which might be needed following serious building damage

- if suitable temporary accommodation is identified in advance, it is important to make regular checks on its continuing availability
- the following options should be considered:
  - accommodation in which to assemble the Disaster Response Team(s)
  - accommodation from which to run core services with emergency teams
  - accommodation for medium or long term use from which temporary services can be run should the library require extensive repairs or is lost
- possible solutions include:
  - assembling the Disaster Response Teams in unaffected areas of the building such as meetings rooms, canteens, rest rooms or storage areas (have at least two options)
  - providing temporary services from other branches in the library system
  - staff working from home
  - listing meetings rooms for hire at local hotels or conferences centres
  - establishing reciprocal arrangements with other local organisations

> Make arrangements with stationers for ordering emergency supplies of essential stationery

See also:
Preparedness. Communication
Preparedness. Computers
Preparedness. Human resources

Preparedness

All staff must be made aware of procedures for raising the alarm and evacuating the building, including evacuation routes, emergency exits, assembly points and who is responsible for ensuring that both public and staff areas are evacuated

- include this training in induction courses
- as well as initial training, refresher courses will be needed at regular intervals
- the term 'staff' should include temporary staff, contract staff and volunteers. All should receive at least basic training with due consideration to any security implications

---

All staff must be trained in the safe and effective use of fire extinguishers, but must be instructed never to tackle any fire at the risk of their own or anyone else's personal safety

- include this training in induction courses
- as well as initial training, refresher courses will be needed at regular intervals
- demonstrations are important - most people have no idea what actually happens when a fire extinguisher goes off!

All staff must know that there is a written disaster control plan, be aware of their own roles and responsibilities in the event of a disaster, and know where emergency equipment and supplies are kept

- include this training in induction courses
- as well as initial training, refresher courses will be needed at regular intervals

---

An awareness of the need for flexibility during a disaster response should be included in training courses

- disasters are by their very nature unpredictable. Staff must, therefore, be able to react quickly whatever the particular circumstances. For example, train staff to deal with 'the effects of water ingress', rather than 'how to deal with a burst pipe'

Continues...

> All staff must be made aware of who is responsible for building and equipment safety, and the procedures for reporting and chasing up any problems

- include this training in induction courses
- as well as initial training, refresher courses will be needed at regular intervals

---

> Target more in-depth training at the Disaster Manager, Disaster Recovery Manager, Disaster Reaction Manager(s), and members of Disaster Response Team(s)

- start with the person(s) responsible for risk assessments and drawing up the disaster control plan
- ensure that the Disaster Manager, Disaster Recovery Manager, Disaster Reaction Manager(s) and members of Disaster Response Teams are wholly familiar with the written disaster control plan, and, in particular, their roles and responsibilities during the reaction and recovery stages
- those responsible for liaison with commercial and other sources of advice, expertise and services need to 'know their language' in order to make rational decisions based on the often conflicting advice they may be given
- according to their roles and responsibilities, staff may need training and guidance on:
     compiling a written disaster control plan
     handling and salvaging different types of damaged materials
     liaison with key personnel within the parent organisation (for example, finance and insurance officers)
     liaison with insurers and loss adjusters
     liaison with the emergency services
     liaison with the media
     liaison with conservators, salvage and restoration companies, emergency equipment suppliers and transportation companies
     providing and organising temporary services
     restoring damaged premises
- any individual training needs should be identified, and suitable training arranged, on the basis of personal experience and previous education and training, as well as roles and responsibilities
- as well as initial training, refresher courses will be needed at regular intervals

Continues...

Preparedness

Training must be realistic	• staff may, for example, be asked to work in the dark, without adequate heating or in water during a disaster and need to practice working in such conditions

Ensure that staff working with computers are aware of emergency backup procedures and other disaster preparedness measures

Carry out practice runs of the disaster control plan and simulations such as desk top exercises to enable staff to familiarise themselves with the plan, and to highlight any omissions or aspects of the plan which do not work as well as intended	• although practice runs are difficult and time consuming to organise, it is simply not possible to know whether or not the written disaster control plan will work properly unless it is tested • involve emergency services, especially local fire services and invite feedback

See also:
Preparedness. Computers
Preparedness. Human resources
Preparedness. Security

Preparedness

| Write a disaster control plan! |

| Keep the plan flexible |

- the plan should offer sufficient guidance to enable a flexible response to any potential disaster situation.

| The plan must be supported by staff awareness raising and training programmes |

| Ensure that the library's plan fits in with any held by its parent organisation or the building in which it is housed |

- the plan must be both organisation- and building-specific
- any existing organisational plan may save time, providing useful information such as sources of advice, expertise and services. Those responsible for writing such a plan will have gained valuable experience, and should be approached for advice

| Organise the plan according to the four stage 'prevention, preparedness, reaction and recovery' model |

- make the plan concise and easy to understand
- include a short policy statement outlining the aims, objectives and scope of the plan
- keep the plan in a loose leaf folder and consider using different coloured paper for each section
- include references to any documentation used in drafting the plan
- include cross-references to relevant building and equipment inspection/maintenance manuals and records
- number pages and include a Contents page. Give page numbers as well as section numbers in the Contents
- indicate the date the plan was completed as a 'footer' on each page. Amend as necessary each time changes are made to the plan (this might mean changing the date on a single page or several). If the plan, or part of it, is significantly revised a new version of it should be created and the footer amended accordingly

Continues...

Preparedness

Include a brief separate or 'pull-out' section with concise, simple, easy to follow instructions for raising the alarm and for immediate use during the reaction stage

- instructions for immediate use during the reaction stage should include:

    Disaster Response Team member(s) to be contacted in the event of a disaster (include office telephone numbers, job titles and the departments or sections in which each works; list names in the order in which they should be contacted, for example, the Disaster Reaction Manager(s) first; for those on call out lists include home telephone numbers, addresses and state whether or not they have their own transport)

    how to contact the emergency services

    electricity and gas suppliers' telephone numbers

    floor plans showing evacuation routes, emergency exits and assembly points

    floor plans showing the location of fire extinguishers, fire-risers, heat and smoke detectors and emergency equipment and supplies

    floor plans showing electrical, water, sewerage, drainage and gas systems highlighting fuse boxes, stopcocks and isolation valves

    floor plans showing items and collections prioritised for salvage

    name(s) and telephone number(s) of first aid officer(s) and location of first aid box(es)

- decide whether or not sensitive information such as staff home telephone numbers and addresses or floor plans showing items and collections prioritised for salvage should be included only in plans held by the Disaster Reaction Manager(s) and those on call out lists on a 'need to know' basis

Continues...

Preparedness

List all library staff with specific disaster management roles and responsibilities	• include the name(s), job title(s), telephone numbers and sections/departments of:
	    the Disaster Manager
	    the Disaster Recovery Manager
	    the Disaster Reaction Manager(s)
	    Disaster Response team members
	    Media Liaison Officer
	    the person(s) responsible for writing the plan
	    the person(s) responsible for reviewing and updating the plan
	    the person(s) responsible for buildings inspections and equipment maintenance
	• include a brief description of each person's roles and responsibilities

List other organisational staff who may need to be contacted in the event of a disaster	• include any 24hr emergency contacts or services within the parent organisation
	• include the name(s), job title(s) and telephone numbers of contacts in:
	    buildings and estates
	    finance
	    insurance
	    media and public relations
	    security

List selected sources of advice, expertise and services	• include details of:
	    contact names, telephone numbers and addresses
	    the services each can offer, and how much they will cost (or at the very least, cost estimates)
	    any service agreements or formal contracts
	• ensure that all these details are kept fully up to date as part of standard review procedures

Provide instructions for Disaster Reaction Managers and Disaster Response Team(s) on handling and salvaging different types of damaged materials	

Continues...

Use flowcharts and other illustrative diagrams to make instructions and procedures easier to understand and follow	• flowcharts are particularly useful for describing procedures such as: 　　raising the alarm 　　contacting members of the Disaster Response Team(s) 　　handling and salvaging damaged materials
Give details of any contingency arrangements which have been made for temporary accommodation and storage for possible use following a more serious disaster	• include: 　　contact names, addresses and telephone numbers 　　type and size of accommodation
Keep copies of the plan in separate, secure locations and state where they can be found in the plan	• the Disaster Manager, Disaster Reaction Manager(s) and Disaster Response Team members should each have two copies of the plan, one of which should be kept at home
Review the plan at least every twelve months. Also review it following refurbishment, changes in building use, building moves and any staff changes which might affect it	• include the name(s), job title(s) and full contact details of the person(s) responsible for reviewing and updating the plan • any amendments or revisions must be authorised by the Disaster Manager • always keep copies of the latest version of the plan on hard and floppy disks. Keep copies of older versions for reference, but score them through or in some other way make it obvious that they are no longer current

Continues...

Preparedness

Include photocopiable disaster report forms and forms for recording items sent for conservation or temporary storage

- copies of these forms should be kept as part of the library's emergency supplies

Indicate how often buildings inspections and equipment maintenance checks should be carried out and keep a record of them in an appendix

Review the plan following a disaster response in order to highlight any aspects of it which may not have worked as well as intended

- include review, final reporting and feedback procedures in the plan

Note:

Considerable guidance on writing a disaster control plan is available in the literature. Although such guidance is extremely helpful, and should be consulted, it is essential that libraries take a pro-active approach to disaster management, designing their own plan which meets their particular circumstances and requirements

All sections of the guidelines should be considered before completing the written disaster control plan

R eaction

4. Reaction

Reaction involves raising the alarm, evacuating the building, instigating initial procedures and activities aimed at protecting undamaged materials, salvaging damaged materials and stabilising the environment

R eaction

If necessary, contact internal and/or external sources of advice, expertise and services

- internal and external sources of advice, expertise and services will already have been identified, consulted and included in the written disaster control plan as part of disaster preparedness activities
- be specific when describing what has happened; for example, do not report two hundred saturated nineteenth century books as 'some wet books'!

If in any doubt regarding the conservation of any valuable and/or irreplaceable damaged items, take expert conservation advice immediately

Be prepared to have to decide between the often conflicting advice given by different experts!

- experts, may have different opinions on particular techniques and approaches, or may not be fully familiar with new developments

Be aware that there will be occasions when quoted response times, emergency equipment delivery times and promises of 24hr service are unlikely to be met because of demand

- weather conditions are often a crucial factor. It may, for example, be extremely difficult to find dehumidifiers in the middle of a hot and humid summer, or a plumber to deal with burst pipes following a thaw in a very cold winter!

Air-conditioning or ventilation systems may need to be shut down manually, if this is not done automatically, in the event of a fire

- if not shut down, air-conditioning and ventilation systems may cause the fire and/or smoke to spread into other parts of the building
- floor plans showing air-conditioning systems will be included in the written disaster control plan

Services such as gas, electricity and water may need to be turned off

- floor plans showing electrical, gas and water systems (with isolation valves and stopcocks highlighted) will be included in the written disaster control plan

Emergency equipment such as dehumidifiers may be needed to return the fabric of the building, and/or its contents or general environment, to acceptable levels of temperature and humidity

Individual items and collections will have been prioritised for salvage on a methodical basis as part of disaster preparedness activities

- it may, however, not always be possible to salvage items in the prioritised order due to prevailing circumstances. For example, access may be denied to structurally unsound areas of the building

If in any doubt, take expert conservation advice on the handling and treatment of damaged items immediately

- different kinds of material will require different treatments
- although instructions on handling and salvaging different materials will be included in written disaster control plans, the right treatment for a particular item may not always be obvious to the non-specialist

See also:
Reaction. Handling and salvaging damaged materials
Recovery. Collections
Recovery. Handling and salvaging damaged materials

R eaction

> The alarm should be raised in accordance with instructions to staff written as part of disaster preparedness planning activities

> As soon as the alarm has been raised, the Disaster Reaction Manager, or designated Disaster Response Team member, must be contacted

- a list of names and contact details will have been prepared as part of disaster preparedness planning activities. Lists will have been kept by telephones, and a copy included in the written disaster control plan

> The Disaster Reaction Manager, or designated Disaster Response Team member, will need to assess the situation and decide on a suitable response

> Other Disaster Response Team members and sources of advice, expertise or services will need to be contacted immediately as required

- sources of advice, expertise or services will be included in the written disaster control plan
- the Disaster Reaction Manager, or the person acting on his or her behalf, may also need to contact staff in other departments within the parent organisation, such as insurance, computing or finance officers, particularly if it is a more serious situation

> Maintain close liaison with the emergency services if called

- in the event of a fire the fire officer in charge will decide when it is safe to enter the building
- the police may control access to the building if a fire is being treated as suspicious
- the emergency services prefer to deal with one person with a good knowledge of the building and its contents and facilities

Continues...

| Keep all staff fully informed of what has happened, what services are unavailable and what temporary arrangements have been made | • do not forget to include staff at other sites or branches |

| Alert staff in other departments of the parent organisation as necessary | • the following departments may need to be alerted: buildings and estates computer department finance office media and public relations security
• following a more serious disaster, these departments will take responsibility for areas of reaction and recovery which come under their remit |

| Mobile telephones will be extremely useful for maintaining communication if land-lines have been lost, or when investigating and dealing with problems in large buildings | • libraries should consider including mobile telephones in their emergency equipment and supplies |

| Any enquiries from the media must be directed to the Media Liaison Officer | • any information given out by the parent organisation's PR department must be given prior clearance by the Media Liaison Officer |

See also:
Reaction. Public relations
Reaction. Service continuity and access
Recovery. Communication
Recovery. Service continuity and access

If necessary, staff working with computers will need to carry out emergency backup procedures

- emergency backup procedures will have been made known to staff as part of disaster preparedness training

If predetermined circumstances prevail, designated staff will need to shut down computer systems, or inform service providers to do so

- documentation to enable faults to be reported and computer systems restored in the absence of the computer manager or other senior computing staff should have been compiled as part of disaster preparedness planning activities

Liaison may be necessary with service providers to implement and manage contingency arrangements

R eaction

The Disaster Response Team(s) will need to take emergency equipment and supplies from disaster trolleys, wheelie-bins or stores and use as them necessary

- replace as soon as possible any emergency equipment and supplies used

The Disaster Reaction Manager may need to make quick spending decisions, and will need the full support of the librarian or finance officer to do so

- the Disaster Reaction Manager may, for example, need to send water damaged archives for freeze/vacuum drying, hire emergency equipment and arrange for temporary storage, all at a time when any delays might prove costly

Always act as if it is the library's money that is being spent, even if an insurance claim has been made. Do not simply assume "the insurance company will pay up"!

- insurers will carefully assess any claims made. They will require proof of losses and good reasons for any money spent

The insurance company may require work to be carried out to a different programme and/or time scale than planned by the library.

- be flexible where possible so that work is undertaken in partnership

Cash may need to be made quickly available for *ad hoc* purchases such as stationery, hiring emergency equipment, transportation and accommodation

- it takes time to replace lost cheque books, and although local companies in particular may want to help, they will also want to be paid

See also:
Reaction. Insurance

The following guidelines on handling and salvaging damaged materials assume that the affected area(s) is/are safe to work in

- the emergency services (if in attendance) will typically decide whether or not an affected area is safe to enter

---

The Disaster Reaction Manager will need to assess priorities for salvaging damaged items, and protecting or removing any items under threat

- individual items and collections will have been prioritised for salvage on a methodical basis as part of disaster preparedness activities. Floor plans showing these prioritised items and collections will have been included in the library's written disaster control plan

---

Protect undamaged materials

- remove any threats, for example, standing water on the floor or high humidity levels
- protect undamaged materials from water and dirt with polythene sheeting

---

The Disaster Reaction Manager will need to organise and instruct Disaster Response Teams as necessary

- in a larger scale disaster or in a larger library - staffing levels permitting - separate teams will be needed for protecting undamaged stock, setting up temporary storage and drying areas, sorting damaged items according to type of material, damage and proposed conservation treatment, cleaning, drying, packing and removing items for storage or treatment
- where disaster salvage and recovery companies have been called in, they will supply additional personnel as the situation demands. The activities of the library's teams and the disaster salvage and recovery company's teams must be coordinated

---

Time will be a major factor when dealing with damaged materials

- the first 48hrs are crucial for the rescue of water-damaged paper materials to prevent mould growth

Continues...

Set up temporary work areas	• for example, clear tables at which to work, space for air drying books • organise appropriate emergency equipment and supplies

If in any doubt, the Disaster Reaction Manager must take expert conservation advice on handling and treating damaged materials	• conservation expertise (whether inside or outside the library), will already have been identified and consulted, and included in the written disaster control plan, as part of disaster preparedness activities • the Disaster Reaction Manager may have to decide between conflicting expert advice

Having taken any necessary advice, the Disaster Reaction Manager will instruct teams to identify and separate materials according to their conservation requirements and degree of damage	• different kinds of material require different treatments. For example,
	• water-damaged books may need to be separated into:
	   those which can be air-dried (books with art/coated papers need interleaving with polythene and blotting paper to prevent pages sticking together)
	   those which require freezing (this stabilises the material, preventing further deterioration, enabling conservation work to be carried out at a later date)
	   those needing to be sent for freeze/vacuum drying (this may be a relatively expensive process, and items for this treatment should be carefully selected, for example, on the basis of their significance and value)
	• fire-damaged paper is extremely delicate and should only be cleaned and treated by experts
	• water-damaged microforms should be immersed in buckets of cold water for later conservation work in the processing laboratory
	• conservation of photographic materials should be left to experts
	• if in any doubt, take expert conservation advice immediately, particularly with regard to drying processes

Continues...

R eaction

Identify any items damaged beyond repair and put them aside for discard. If a damaged item can be replaced easily at a cost less than, or the same as, estimated conservation costs then it too should be discarded	• if in any doubt, retain items and take expert advice • remember to include all the costs involved in processing new stock when assessing replacement costs, rather than simply the purchase price • if an insurance claim has been made, do not dispose of any damaged items until advised to do so by insurers or agents acting on their behalf such as loss adjusters

Always take care when cleaning, moving, packing and sorting items	• for example:
	    do not over-pack crates
	    do not pull apart books or papers which are stuck together
	    do not unwind or separate microforms
	    wrap books in vellum bindings in crepe bandages to avoid distortion before wrapping in polythene bags
	    wrap sodden books and papers in polythene bags
	    label each crate with an identifying mark and record its contents

Remove damaged items from disaster area(s) for conservation treatment	• keep a record of all items sent for conservation treatment. Record:
	    where they are sent
	    the date they are sent
	    the treatment required
	    their shelf positions
	• photocopiable recording forms should be included in the written disaster control plan

Continues...

Note:

Common causes of damage to library materials are fire, soot and water. Even where fire is the cause of the incident, water damage often follows as a result of extinguishing the fire. The type and degree of damage will vary according to the cause and scale of the incident and materials affected.

It will not always be possible to carry out handling and salvage activities according to predetermined priorities. Following a more serious disaster, for example, higher priority items may be in structurally unsafe areas, and have to be left until later.

There is considerable guidance in the literature on the various methods and techniques of handling and treating different kinds of damaged library materials. A few illustrative examples of these methods and techniques are provided above. Items in the bibliography contain more in-depth detail and advice and will need to be consulted.

It is important to recognise that whilst reading about these methods and techniques will be helpful, it is no substitute for practical experience of handling these materials. 'Hands-on' training sessions involving sorting and dealing with damaged materials are essential, as is taking expert advice.

See also:
Reaction. Collections
Recovery. Collections

People's health and safety must be the primary concern of all staff during the reaction to any disaster, no matter what threats there may be to collections, buildings, contents or facilities

- any necessary evacuation procedures will be put into effect as soon as the alarm is raised

In the event of a fire, the fire officer in charge will decide when it is safe to enter the building

The Disaster Reaction Manager must ensure that the correct protective clothing is provided for staff working in dirty and/or dangerous conditions, and that this clothing is worn at all times

- if in any doubt regarding the correct protective clothing that should be worn, take expert advice

Ensure that no one is in danger of electrocution from the mains or any other electricity supply, particularly if water is present. Switch off the supply immediately should there be even the slightest danger

- the whereabouts of fuse boxes and mains switches will be on floor plans included in the written disaster control plan

Continues...

Water may be contaminated by sewage or other matter, and may contain harmful bacteria or viruses	• if in any doubt regarding water quality or the protective clothing that should be worn, take expert advice • even when water is declared safe to work in, the Disaster Reaction Manager must ensure that protective clothing, such as rubber boots and overalls, is worn at all times by staff standing in, or wading through, water
Following a fire, the air will be contaminated with soot particles, which may contain harmful materials such as plastics or asbestos	• air quality should be tested at the earliest opportunity and then regularly monitored by health and safety experts to ascertain whether or not a particular area is safe to work in (and in case of subsequent litigation by staff) • even when environmental conditions are declared safe to work in, the Disaster Reaction Manager must ensure that staff wear protective clothing, such as face masks and cloth gloves all times
When handling organic materials such as paper, parchment or vellum, staff may need to wear masks as protection against fungal or bacterial organisms	
Always be careful when lifting anything heavy	• adopt correct lifting techniques to avoid back and other injuries • crates of wet books are heavy - do not over-pack

R eaction

The Disaster Reaction Manager will organise and instruct Disaster Response Teams as necessary

- the Disaster Reaction Manager will need to be flexible as staff in Disaster Response Teams may be on holiday, out of the office or engaged on duties from which they cannot immediately be released
- staff not assigned to Disaster Response Teams may be needed in the event of a more serious disaster; this will be a matter for the librarian, or other senior manager, to decide on at the time

The Disaster Reaction Manager must write a report on the actions taken in response to every disaster - no matter how small - stating when and why they were taken

- writing a report on even the smallest disaster can alert the library to any minor recurring problems which can then be dealt with before they become more serious
- a reaction report will be a useful *aide memoire* when reviewing and assessing the actions taken as part of standard review procedures, and when making an insurance claim
- following a more serious disaster, a member of staff may need to 'shadow' the Disaster Reaction Manager to record and comment on actions taken
- photographic or video records of a disaster response can be extremely useful when reviewing actions

Reacting to even a minor disaster can be hard and dirty work. Ensure that staff have regular breaks with refreshments

- if possible, organise relief teams

Maintain staff morale!

- staff need to know that their efforts are recognised and appreciated

143

R eaction

Insurers should be contacted
as soon as it becomes apparent that a
claim is likely to be made

- insurers will be contacted either directly, or through finance departments, according to standard organisational procedures
- following a more serious loss, the insurers may appoint loss adjusters with whom the library will have to negotiate

Whenever possible, discuss spending
options with insurers before deciding on
a particular course of action

See also:
Reaction. Finance

144

R eaction

If services are affected keep users fully informed of what has happened, what services are unavailable, what temporary arrangements have been made, what is being done to remedy the situation and when any affected services are likely to be restored	• be realistic about restoration of services • consider preparing proformas on which this information can be recorded and kept on enquiry points • initially, most users will be sympathetic if apprised of the situation, but be aware that this sympathy may not last for very long!
If the media become involved, be sure to get them 'on your side' as quickly as possible	• direct all media enquiries to the Media Liaison Officer to maintain control and consistency over what is said • ensure that staff are aware that they should not speak to the media themselves, but direct all enquiries to the Media Liaison Officer
The Media Liaison Officer must be sufficiently well-informed about the current situation to answer satisfactorily any media enquiries	• the media will not be fobbed off with unhelpful or obstructive answers - they will simply turn to other, 'unofficial' sources • the Media Liaison Officer should be in regular contact with the Disaster Reaction Manager
The Media Liaison Officer should prepare a brief statement for the media	• it is essential to maintain control over what is said, and to ensure consistency

See also:
Reaction. Communication
Recovery. Public relations

R eaction

> If in attendance, the emergency services will control access to the library

> Assess whether or not there are any measures which need to be taken to prevent unauthorised access in order to ensure people's safety and to stop theft

- if necessary security can be maintained by:
  - roping-off the affected area(s)
  - posting security guards
  - issuing identification badges to staff and other authorised personnel
  - issue authorised personnel with passwords and change them often

See also:
Recovery. Security

R eaction

Any adverse effects on service continuity and access must be minimised

If necessary, set up a team with responsibility for organising and implementing temporary services

- users will need to be kept fully informed of what has happened, what services are unavailable, what temporary arrangements have been made, what is being done to remedy the situation and when affected services are likely to be restored
- if possible (that is, where staff numbers allow), members of this team should not be involved in other disaster reaction or recovery work

Be aware that most users, having no perception of the complexities of the situation, will expect normal services to be resumed very quickly

See also:
Reaction. Communication
Recovery. Service continuity and access

R eaction

All staff should have been made aware of their own roles and responsibilities during induction and specialised training courses

- staff will still need to be flexible in their approach in order to respond quickly to unforeseen circumstances

R eaction

Be flexible!

- the plan provides vital information, but is not (nor could it be) a step-by-step guide to dealing with each and every disaster situation

---

Keep a record of all actions taken in response to a disaster, stating when and why they were taken. Review these actions, highlighting any mistakes which may have been made and any aspects of the plan which did not work as well as intended

- the Disaster Reaction Manager should have written a report on all actions taken in response to a disaster, in order to facilitate such as a review
- photographic or video records of a disaster response can be extremely useful when reviewing actions

R ecovery

5. Recovery

Recovery involves post-reaction procedures and activities
aimed at restoring buildings, collections, contents,
facilities and services, and implementing any necessary
measures to ensure service continuity and access

> Always take expert conservation advice as soon as possible on any valuable and/ or irreplaceable damaged items

- conservation expertise (whether inside or outside the library), will already have been identified, and included in the written disaster control plan, as part of disaster preparedness activities
- there may also need to be long term liaison with conservators regarding materials which have been frozen for treatment at a later date

> Be prepared to have to decide between the often conflicting advice given by different experts!

- be aware that commercial salvage companies and disaster recovery services have a financial interest which may colour their perceptions. Investigation of their claims to expertise and experience as part of disaster preparedness activities will govern the choice of whose advice to follow

The following guidelines on buildings, contents and facilities assume that the affected area(s) is/are safe to work in, and that appropriate security precautions have been taken

- if in attendance, the emergency services will control access to the site. Buildings, contents and facilities recovery can begin only when the library is considered safe to re-enter

Internal and/or external sources of advice, expertise and services will need to be contacted based on an initial assessment of any damage

- sources of advice, expertise and services will already have been identified, consulted and included in the written disaster control plan as part of disaster preparedness activities

Mould growth must be prevented or, if discovered, removed as soon as possible. Use dehumidifiers (with fans to increase air-circulation) to reduce high humidity levels

- remove all library stock from the affected area(s)
- dry or remove wet carpeting
- check temperature and humidity levels at frequent and regular intervals for a period of twelve months
- consider washing shelves, walls, floors and ceilings with fungicide, but only after taking expert advice
- keep the affected area(s) as well-ventilated as possible. For example, (security permitting) windows may be kept open during warm, dry weather, while internal doors should be left open during damp or wet weather
- vacuum regularly
- check regularly and thoroughly for signs of mould - look behind shelves and under carpets and floors!
- obtain expert advice, for example, from the parent organisation's buildings and estates department, before declaring the area(s) free from mould and returning stock

Any necessary fumigation should only be carried out by experts

- environmental specialists should already have been identified, consulted and included in the written disaster control plan as part of disaster preparedness activities

The Disaster Reaction Manager, or an appointed member of staff, may need to act on the library's behalf in negotiations with salvage and restoration companies, conservators and binders

- following a more serious disaster, a Disaster Recovery Manager may have been appointed to carry out these and other longer term activities
- always deal with the reputable companies and individuals already identified as part of disaster preparedness activities (in addition to any appointed by the insurers). Beware of industrial cleaning companies offering 'cheap deals' to take the library's books away for cleaning

Establish on-site treatment areas for drying and other conservation work, and carry out as much work as possible on-site

- tables may be needed for air-drying, and cold air fans and polythene sheeting for making wind tunnels

Move sorted undamaged items from interim to temporary storage areas as necessary

- clarify cover for transportation and storage costs with insurers. Insurers may only pay for the initial removal of items to temporary storage, and not for any subsequent moves, so the temporary accommodation must be right first time!

Move sorted damaged items to binders, conservators and/or salvage and restoration companies as necessary

Be aware of any security risks when transporting and temporarily storing stock

- insurers, in particular, will need assurances regarding the security of any valuable and/or irreplaceable items kept in temporary storage

R ecovery

See also:
Reaction. Collections
Reaction. Handling and salvaging damaged materials
Recovery. Handling and salvaging damaged materials

Close liaison with the emergency services will be necessary until they leave the site

Keep all staff fully informed of what is happening, what is being done to remedy the situation and when any affected services are likely to be restored

- in particular, following a more serious disaster, staff will want to know how their own situation is affected. They may need reassurance regarding job security and salary payments
- give staff a telephone number which they can contact for up to date information
- do not forget to keep staff who have been asked to remain at home fully informed. Make sure that they do not feel 'left out'

Keep staff in other departments of the parent organisation fully informed as necessary

If telephone land-lines have been lost, restoring at least one direct line with fax facilities will be a major priority

- mobile telephones will be extremely useful in this situation

See also:
Reaction. Communication
Recovery. Public relations

Ensure that predetermined emergency
procedures are put into place and that
they are meeting service
requirements

- liaison may be necessary with service providers, network managers and internal computer departments

Liaison may be necessary with suppliers
to replace any lost software and
hardware

- replacement may take a considerable amount of time!
- renting hardware should be considered as an option until the library is absolutely clear on what it needs (it may, for example, take the opportunity to upgrade)

> The Disaster Reaction Manager, or an appointed member of staff, may need to contact emergency equipment suppliers to hire equipment not available in-house

- following a more serious disaster, a Disaster Recovery Manager may have been appointed to carry out these and other longer term activities
- always deal with the reputable companies and individuals already identified as part of disaster preparedness activities

> Replace as soon as possible any emergency equipment and supplies taken from stores, disaster trolleys or wheelie-bins used during the reaction stage

- the effectiveness of any emergency equipment and supplies used, however, should be assessed as part of post-disaster review procedures (as well as being assessed as part of annual review procedures)

Beware ambulance chasers!	• although following a more serious disaster the library will receive many offers of genuine help from within and outside the profession, there will still be many who will see it as a moneymaking opportunity. For example:
	    emergency equipment and transportation charges may be hiked up
	    temporary storage may be offered at inflated rents
	    industrial cleaners may offer to clean and restore fire and soot-damaged books at 'bargain prices' (only to damage them further in the process)

Cash may need to be made quickly available for *ad hoc* purchases such as stationery, hiring emergency equipment, transportation and accommodation	• it takes time to replace lost cheque books, and although local companies in particular may want to help, they will also want to be paid • libraries in smaller organisations, in particular, may experience cash-flow problems
If an insurance claim has been made, do not incur other than nominal costs without the insurer's approval (or the approval of an agent acting on their behalf, such as a loss adjuster)	• always act as if it is the library's money being spent, even if an insurance claim has been made!

See also:
Recovery. Insurance

R ecovery

Ensure that environmental conditions such as temperature and relative humidity are stabilised at suitable levels before returning items to shelves

- ensure that shelves are clean, dry and free from mould

Items will need to be carefully checked on their return following conservation treatment

- ensure that conservation work has been carried out to agreed specifications

See also:
Reaction. Handling and salvaging damaged materials
Recovery. Collections

R ecovery

> People's health and safety must remain
> the primary concern of all staff during
> recovery from any disaster

Note:

Continue to be aware of the health and safety requirements outlined in Reaction. Health and Safety.

R ecovery

Maintain staff morale!	• even a minor disaster can mean hard and dirty work, and staff need to know that their efforts are recognised and appreciated. Maintaining morale will become even more important, however, should the scale of the disaster mean a prolonged recovery period • ensure that staff get regular breaks with refreshments. If possible, organise relief teams. • ensure that staff wear old clothing when working in dirty conditions and warm clothing when working in cold and/ or damp conditions (in addition to any necessary protective clothing) • ensure prompt payment of any overtime payments, or arrange for time to be taken off *in lieu*
Make counselling available to all staff immediately following a disaster and in the longer term if required	• be aware that staff often have a deep personal attachment to the library and its collections, and may experience a deep sense of loss following a disaster • do not forget to offer counselling to part-time or contract staff who can easily be overlooked
Following a more serious disaster, develop a good, supportive team spirit to help staff to come to terms with what has happened	• get staff together in the morning before they start work, and at the end of the day before they go home, to air their views and discuss how work is progressing
The Disaster Reaction Manager must write a report on all actions taken during the recovery period, stating when and why they were taken	• a reaction report will be a useful *aide memoire* when reviewing and assessing the actions taken as part of standard review procedures, and when making an insurance claim • following a more serious disaster, a member of staff may need to 'shadow' the Disaster Reaction Manager to record and comment on actions taken • photographic or video records of a disaster response can be extremely useful when reviewing actions

Insurers will carefully assess any claims made and will require proof of losses and good reasons for any money spent	• do not dispose of any damaged or lost items, whether stock or contents, until advised to do so by insurers • keep photographic or video records of any damaged or lost stock or contents
Discuss spending options with insurers before going ahead with a particular decision	• insurers will need to know why an apparently 'more expensive' option was chosen before agreeing the claim • loss adjusters, if appointed, can discuss spending options if this is more convenient
Quickly develop an open and honest working relationship with insurers, and, if appointed, agents acting on their behalf such as loss adjusters	• following a more serious disaster, insurers will appoint loss adjusters to mitigate their losses and organise and coordinate recovery
Pay particular attention to insurance cover relating to the transportation and temporary storage of stock and other items	• potential problems may arise, for example, if stock is kept in parked lorries overnight, or if temporary storage facilities have inadequate security
Put together an insurance claim based on catalogues and inventories of office furniture and equipment	• inventories should have been compiled as part of disaster preparedness activities

Continues...

Recovery

See also:
Recovery. Finance

R ecovery

Keep users, the media and any other interested parties aware of what is happening as necessary

- senior managers in the parent organisation, elected members or local politicians may need to be briefed and kept informed
- provide, good, well-organised, library-managed photographic and interviewing opportunities; do not allow the media uncontrolled access

The Media Liaison Officer must keep staff in the parent organisation's media and public relations departments fully informed, but must still retain control over any information given out

Local media can be very helpful following a more serious disaster

- local radio, for example, may help public libraries to keep their users informed about temporary services and contingency arrangements for returning borrowed items

Local and national media can be used to launch appeals for replacing lost local history items

See also:
Reaction. Public Relations
Recovery. Communication

R ecovery

If in attendance, the emergency services will control access to the site, but security may still be a problem after they have left

Continue to take any measures necessary to prevent unauthorised access

See also:
Reaction. Security

R ecovery

Appropriate management structures and teams with clearly defined responsibilities will need to be established according to prevailing circumstances

- both individuals and teams will need to be able to react to events as they unfold
- staff not involved in recovery work such as handling and salvaging damaged materials may be assigned to teams responsible for maintaining service continuity and access

Short, medium and longer term contingency arrangements for service continuity and access may be necessary

- procedures may need to be established for the redirection and receipt of mail and other deliveries
- newspapers, periodicals and book or equipment orders may need to be cancelled or redirected
- contingency arrangements may be needed to:
  provide temporary services
  maintain computer and telecommunications services
  provide temporary accommodation for staff and equipment
  provide temporary accommodation for stock and/or contents

Set a timetable against which targets for restoring services can be measured

Consider how the disaster may affect any of the library's business plans

See also:
Reaction. Service continuity and access

A thorough review and analysis of the disaster response should be carried out and anything learned incorporated in subsequent training courses and sessions

- those who have been involved in a disaster response, often consider it to have been the best possible learning experience!

Practical training sessions in particular can benefit greatly from the lessons learned during a disaster response

A full report of any disaster response, however minor, should be written	• the Disaster Manager should see all reports. This will enable the Disaster Manager to identify any common or underlying problems and causes for concern that may not be apparent to those working in individual departments or sections of the library

A thorough review of the plan should be carried out following any disaster response	• reviewing the plan should be looked at positively as a learning process, and not as an exercise in 'looking for faults' or 'someone to blame' • hindsight may reveal that: mistakes have been made aspects of the plan have not worked as well as anticipated omissions in the plan

The Disaster Reaction Manager should include all those involved in the disaster response in review procedures	• initial group 'debriefing sessions' are useful for analysing events and actions, and obtaining the views of staff

Amend and/or add to the plan as necessary

6. Bibliography

This is a select bibliography; it is not an exhaustive bibliography of disaster management. It contains items recommended by interviewees and/or which the authors have themselves found useful. The emphasis is on up to date British material supplemented with additional items as appropriate. Many of the items in the bibliography themselves include references to other useful sources, British and international, not included here.

The bibliography is arranged according to the headings used in the guidelines with additional subheadings for some more specific topics. It is recommended that readers begin with items under 'General guidance'. Items in this section provide a general overview as well as information on specific topics. For instance, advice on handling and salvaging materials can be found in Ashman, 1995 (*Salvaging water-damaged materials*, pp. 25-40; *Conservation*, pp. 41-47) and Buchanan, 1988 (*Disaster recovery, water*, pp. 71-90; *Disaster recovery, fire*, pp. 93-103) both of which are included under 'General guidance'.

Bibliography

National Preservation Office. *Disaster planning: a bibliography*. London: NPO, 1993.

Buildings, contents and facilities

BS 826. *Specification for steel single tier bolted shelving (angle upright type)*. London: BSI, 1978.

BS 5454. *Recommendations for storage and exhibition of archival documents*. London: BSI, 1989.

National Preservation Office. *Controlling your library environment*. London: NPO, 1992. (Videocassette.)

Computing

Benbow, Gary. The seven myths of computer recovery. *International Journal of Information Resource Management*, 3(4), 1992, pp. 29-31.

Boyd, John. Disaster recovery plans: the Nottinghamshire experience. *Managing Information*, 1(7/8), July/August 1994, pp. 33-35.

BS 7799. *Code of practice for information security management*. London: BSI, 1995.

CCTA (Government Centre for Information Systems). *An introduction to business continuity management*. London: HMSO, 1995. (IT Infrastructure Library.)

Davies, J. Eric. Lock, bolts and bars - real and virtual: computer security. *Managing Information*, 1(7/8), July/August 1994, pp. 28-32.

Edwards, Bruce. Developing a successful network disaster recovery plan. *Information Management and Computer Security*, 2(3), 1994, pp. 37-42.

Fitzgerald, Kevin J. Risk analysis: ten years on. *Information Management and Computer Security*, 1(5), 1993, pp. 23-31.

IBM Report in Association with Loughborough University and the Computing Services Association. Up the creek? - the business perils of computer failure. *Foresight*, July 1994, pp. 6-12.

Learn, Larry L. Diversity: two are not cheaper than one! (A look at facilities disaster avoidance.) *Library Hi Tech News*, January/February 1992, pp. 17-22.

Lincoln, Alan Jay. Computer security. *Library and Archival Security*, 11(1), 1991, pp. 157-171.

McAteer, Jon. Worst case scenario. *LAN Magazine*, July 1995, pp. 145-152.

Oxley, S.T. Security of electronic information. *Perspectives in Information Management*, 3(1), 1993, pp. 5-18.

Rowley, Jennifer. Is your computer system secure? *Managing Information*, 2(7/8), July/August 1995, pp. 38-39.

Solms, R. von, Solms, S.H. von and Caelli, W.J. A model for information security management. *Information Management and Computer Security*, 1(3), 1993, pp. 12-17.

Turner, Rollo. Computers and disasters: putting your PC in the recovery position. *Managing Information*, 1(7/8), July/August 1994, pp. 38-40.

Willcocks L. and Margetts, H. Risk assessment and information systems. *European Journal of Information Systems*. 3(2), 1994, pp. 127-138.

Cooperative initiatives

DePew, John N. *Statewide Disaster Preparedness and Recovery Program for Florida Libraries*. Champaign, Illinois: University of Illinois Graduate School of Library and Information Science, February 1989. (Occasional Papers no. 185.)

Jilovsky, Cathie. CAVAL: a cooperative approach to library disaster management. In, Howell, Alan, Mansell, Heather and Roubos-Bennett, Marion (compilers). *Redefining disasters: a decade of counter-disaster planning. Papers submitted by speakers, Wednesday 20-Friday 22 September 1995, State Library of New South Wales, Sydney, Australia.* Sydney: Conservation Access, State Library of New South Wales, 1995, pp. 69-90.

Safran, Franciska. and Vaughan, Barbara. *The charting of the Western New York Disaster Preparedness Network.* Conservation Administration News, 61, April 1995, pp. 10-13.

Counselling

Pember, Margaret E. The psycho-social (P-S) factor in counter-disaster planning: the human element. In, Howell, Alan, Mansell, Heather and Roubos-Bennett, Marion (compilers). *Redefining disasters: a decade of counter-disaster planning. Papers submitted by speakers, Wednesday 20-Friday 22 September 1995, State Library of New South Wales, Sydney, Australia.* Sydney: Conservation Access, State Library of New South Wales, 1995, pp. 199-206.

Disaster experiences

Davis, Miriam. Disaster management. *The Law Librarian*, 26(3), September 1995, pp. 406-409.

Green, Kevin. The case of the Pilkington Technology Centre fire. *Aslib Information*, 21(2), February 1993, pp. 72-75.

Hayman, David. The Norwich Central Library fire. *Survive!*, May 1995, pp. 22-23.

Kennedy, Jean. Norfolk Record Office fire: an initial report. *Journal of the Society of Archivists*, 16(1), Spring 1995, pp. 3-6.

Raper, Diane. Having a flood? *The Law Librarian*, 19(3), December 1988, pp. 85-88.

Saunders, Margaret. How a library picked up the pieces after IRA blast. *Library Association Record*, 95(2), February 1993, pp. 100-101.

Salmon, Robert. Bank calls on lab to restore water-damaged microfilm. *International Journal of Micrographics and Optical Technology*, 11(2), 1993, pp. 65-67.

Schnare, Robert E. and Curtis, Marilyn D. Fire aftermath and the recovery process. *Conservation Administration News*, 35, October 1988, pp. 1-2, 22.

Thorburn, Georgine. Library fire and flood - successful salvage, but beware of the cowboy. *Aslib Information*, 21(2), February 1993, pp.76-78.

Wise, Christine. The flood and afterwards: a new beginning for the Fawcett Library. *Library Conservation News*, 48, Autumn 1995, pp. 1-2.

Emergency equipment and supplies

Paper Conservation News. Institute of Paper Conservation, 1976- . Quarterly.

Weber, Jerry (ed.). *The directory of suppliers: a comprehensive list of supplies and services for all preservation and conservation needs in archives, museums and libraries*. 4th ed. Preservation and Conservation Group of the Society of Archivists, 1994.

Fire prevention

Bailey, Sir Alan, Insall, Donald and Kilshaw, Philip. *Fire protection measures for the royal palaces*. London: HMSO, 1993.

Cote, William C. A plan for the future. *Library and Archival Security*, 9(3/4), 1989, pp. 89-93.

Cote, William C. Are you truly prepared? *Library and Archival Security*, 9(2), 1989, pp. 67-69.

Cote, William C. Controlling the human element. *Library and Archival Security*, 10(1), 1990, pp. 67-75.

Fire prevention on construction sites. The Joint Code of Practice on the Protection from Fire of Construction

Sites and Buildings Undergoing Renovation. Birmingham: The Building Employers Confederation, The Loss Prevention Council, The National Contractors' Group with the support of The Association of British Insurers, The Chief and Assistant Chief Fire Officers Association and The London Fire Brigade, 1992.

Fire Protection Association. *Construction site fire prevention checklist. A guide for insurers, surveyors and construction industry professionals*. London, FPA, 1994. (Prepared for use alongside *Fire prevention on construction sites. The Joint Code of Practice on the Protection from Fire of Construction Sites and Buildings Undergoing Renovation*.)

Fire Protection Association. *Good housekeeping checklist for industry*. London: FPA, September 1991. (Leaflet.)

Kidd, Stewart (ed.). *Heritage under fire: a guide to the protection of historic buildings*. 2nd ed. London: Fire Protection Association, 1995.

Loss Prevention Certification Board. *Approved fire and security products and services: a specifiers guide*. London: Loss Prevention Council, 1995.

Pearson, B.P. *An inquiry into the fire at the Norwich Central Library on the 1st August 1994*. Norwich: Norfolk County Council, 1995. (The Pearson Report.)

General guidance

Anderson, Hazel and McIntyre, John E. *Planning manual for disaster control in Scottish libraries and record offices*. Edinburgh: National Library of Scotland, 1985.

Ashman, John. *Disaster planning for library and information services*. London: Aslib, 1995. (Aslib Know How Series.)

Baillie, Jeavons, Doig, Judith and Jilovsky, Cathie (eds.). *Disaster in libraries: prevention and control*. 2nd ed. Melbourne: CAVAL, 1994.

Buchanan, Sally. *Disaster planning, preparedness and recovery for libraries and archives: a RAMP study with guidelines*. (PGI-88/WS/6). Paris: General Information Programme and UNISIST, United Nations Educational, Scientific and Cultural Organisation, 1988.

CoOL (Conservation On-line). a full text database of conservation information, a project of the Preservation Department of Stanford University Libraries. <URL: http://palimpsest.stanford.edu/index.shtml>

Cunha, George Martin. Disaster planning and a guide to recovery resources. *Library Technology Reports*, 28(5), 1992, pp. 533-624.

Donnelly, Helene. Disaster planning strategy review. *Records Management Bulletin*, 58, October 1993, pp. 15-17.

Elliott, Lynn. Disaster control planning - a review and case study. In, Harris, Colin (ed.). *The new university library: issues for the '90s and beyond. Essays in honour of Ian Rogerson*. London: Taylor Graham, 1994, pp. 108-119.

Eppard, Philip B. Draft guidelines for the management and preservation of electronic text documents. *Records*

Management Bulletin, 72, February 1996, pp. 4-10.

England, C. and Evans, K. *Disaster management for libraries: planning and process.* Toronto: Canadian Library Association, 1988.

Fortson, Judith. *Disaster planning and recovery: a how-to-do-it manual for librarians and archivists.* New York: Neal-Schuman, 1992. (How-to-do-it Manuals for Libraries no. 21.)

George, Susan C. *Emergency planning and management in college libraries.* Chicago: Association of College and Research Libraries, 1994. (CLIP Note no. 17.)

Gibson, Gerald D. Emergency preparedness and disaster recovery in audiovisual collections. *IASA Journal*, 4, November 1994, pp. 13-18.

Hadgraft, Nicholas. Disaster planning in small libraries. *Bulletin of the Association of British Theological and Philosophical Libraries*, 2(6), November 1989, pp. 21-33.

Howell, Alan, Mansell, Heather and Roubos-Bennett, Marion (compilers). *Redefining disasters: a decade of counter-disaster planning. Papers submitted by speakers Wednesday 20-Friday 22 September 1995, State Library of New South Wales, Sydney, Australia.* Sydney: Conservation Access, State Library of New South Wales, 1995.

Hyams, David. *The guide to disaster recovery planning.* Oxford: MRC Business Information Group, 1993.

Joseph, G.W. and Couturier, G.W. Essential management activities to support effective disaster planning. *International Journal of Information Management*, 13(5) October 1993, pp. 315-325.

Lancaster, John M. Disaster control planning. In, Kenny, Geraldine (ed.). *A reading guide to the preservation of library collections.* London: Library Association, 1991, pp. 63-71.

Langelier, Gilles and Wright, Sandra. Contingency planning for cartographic archives. *Archivaria*, 13, Winter 1981-82, pp. 47-58.

Matthews, Graham. Disaster management: controlling the plan. *Managing Information*, 1(7/8), July/August 1994, pp. 24-27.

McIntyre, J.E. Action planning for disaster. *Refer*, 5(4), Autumn 1989, pp. 1-7.

McIntyre, John. Disaster control planning. *Serials*, 1(2), July 1988, pp. 42-46.

National Preservation Office. *If disaster strikes!* London: NPO, 1988. (Videocassette.)

Skepastianu, Maria and Whiffin, Jean I. *Library disaster planning: prepared for the IFLA Section on Conservation and Preservation.* The Hague: IFLA, 1995. (Leaflet.)

Tregarthen Jenkin, Ian. *Disaster planning and preparedness: an outline disaster control plan.* London: British Library, 1987. (British Library Information Guide 5.)

Virando, Jacqueline A. *Disaster recovery planning and resources for records managers and librarians.* Silver Spring, Maryland: Association for Information and Image Management, 1991. (AIIM Resource Report.)

Glossary

National Preservation Office. *Preservation policies. Glossary*. London: NPO, February 1992. (Leaflet.)

Handling and salvaging damaged materials

Harvey, Christopher. The treatment of flood-damaged photographic material at the Perth Museum and Art Gallery, Scotland. *Paper Conservation News*, 76, December 1995, pp. 8-12.

Kovacic, Ellen Siegel and Wolfson, Laurel Sturman. Moldbusters!! *Conservation Administration News*, 50, July 1992, pp. 6-7, 28.

Shapkina, Larissa B. et al. Restoring book paper and drying books after a disaster. *Restaurator*, 13(2), pp. 47-57.

Sterlini, Philippa. Surface cleaning products and their effects on paper. *Paper Conservation News*, 76, December 1995, pp. 3-7.

Health and safety

Doig, Judith. Evacuation procedures for libraries. *Australasian College Libraries*, 7(1), March 1989, pp. 13-16.

Donnelly, Helene and Heaney, Martin. Disaster planning - a wider approach. *Aslib Information*, 21(2), February 1993, pp. 69-71.

Health and Safety Commission. *Management of health and safety at work. (Management of Health and Safety at Work Regulations 1992)*. London: HMSO, 1992. (Approved code of practice L21.)

Health and Safety Commission. *Workplace health, safety and welfare. (Workplace (Health, Safety and Welfare) Regulations 1992)*. London: HMSO, 1992. (Approved code of practice and guidance L24.)

Health and Safety Executive. *Manual handling. (Manual Handling Operations Regulations 1992)*. London: HMSO, 1992. (Guidance on regulations L23.)

Health and Safety Executive. *Memorandum of guidance on the Electricity at Work Regulations 1989*. London: HMSO, 1989. (Health and safety series booklet. HS(R) 25.)

Health and Safety Executive. *Personal protective equipment at work. (Personal Protective Equipment at Work Regulations 1992)*. London: HMSO, 1992. (Guidance on regulations L25.)

Home Office/Scottish Home and Health Department. *Fire safety at work*. London: HMSO, 1989.

Howie, F. (ed.). *Safety in museums and galleries*. London: Butterworths, 1987.

Simpson, Diana and Simpson, W. Gordon (eds.). *The COSHH regulations: a practical guide*. Cambridge: Royal Society of Chemistry, 1991.

Insurance and risk management

Berges, Cherry. Risk management: the unrecognized necessity. *Rural Libraries*, 1, 1993, pp. 53-66.

Brawner, Lee B. Insurance and risk management for libraries. *Public Library Quarterly*, 13(1), 1993, pp. 5-15. (First part of a two-part article.)

Brawner, Lee B. Insurance and risk management for libraries. *Public Library Quarterly*, 13(2), 1993, pp. 29-34. (Second part of a two-part article.)

Marshall, Vanessa. Assessing and managing risks to your collections. Report on the Leicester workshop. *Paper Conservation News*, 76, December 1995, pp. 17-18.

Ungarelli, Donald L. Are our libraries safe from losses? *Library and Archival Security*, 9(1), 1989, pp. 45-49.

Waller, Robert. Conservation risk assessment: a strategy for managing resources for preventive conservation. In, Roy, Ashok and Smith, Perry (eds.). *Preventive conservation practice, theory and research. Preprints of the contributions to the Ottawa Congress, 12-16 September 1994.* London: International Institute for Conservation of Historic and Artistic Works, 1994, pp. 12-16.

Waller, Robert. Risk management applied to preventive conservation. In, Rose, C.L., Hawks, C.A. and Genoways H.H. (eds.). *Storage of natural history collections: a preventive conservation approach.* Iowa City: Society for the Preservation of Natural History Collections, 1996, pp. 21-28.

Security

BS 8220: Part 2: 1995. *Guide for security of buildings against crime. Part 2. Offices and shops.* London: BSI, 1995.

Burrows, John and Cooper, Diane. *Theft and loss from UK libraries: a national survey.* London: Home Office Police Department, 1992. (Police Research Group Crime Prevention Unit Series: Paper no. 37.)

Home Office. *Bombs - protecting people and property: a guide for small businesses.* London: Home Office Public Relations Branch, March 1994. (Leaflet.)

Home Office. *Bombs - protecting people and property: a handbook for managers and security officers.* London: Home Office Public Relations Branch, 1994.

National Preservation Office. *Designing out crime.* London: NPO, 1996. (Security Matters, 3.) (Leaflet.)

National Preservation Office. *Library security: who cares?* London: NPO, 1990. (Videocassette.)

Thomas, D.L. *Study on control of security and storage of holdings: a RAMP study with guidelines.* (PGI-86/WS/23). Paris: UNESCO, 1987.

Training

Butler, Randall and Davis, Sheryl. IELDRN stages disaster recovery workshop. *Conservation Administration*

News, 40, January 1990, pp. 1-3.

Crane, Marilyn and Davis, Sheryl. The practice of disaster response. *Conservation Administration News*, 55, October 1993, pp. 8-9.

Library Conservation News. National Preservation Office, 1983- . Quarterly.

Matthews, Graham and Eden, Paul. *Disaster management training in libraries.* Library Review, 1996, 45(1), pp. 30-38.

Moore, Tony. Planning and training for a major disaster. *Intersec*, 4(10), October 1994, pp. 329-331.

Page, Julie A. Exercising your disaster plans. A tabletop drill. *Conservation Administration News*, 54, July 1993, pp. 8-9.

Written disaster control plans

Co-operative Action by Victorian Academic Libraries (CAVAL). *Disaster recovery: a model plan for libraries and information centres.* Melbourne: CAVAL, 1993. (With computer disk and manual. Plan in wordprocessor format for customisation by individual libraries. Available in three formats: MS Word for the Macintosh 5.0, MS Word for Windows 2.0 and 6.0 and Wordperfect 5.1 and 6.0.)

National Preservation Office/Riley Dunn and Wilson. *Keeping our words: the 1988 National Preservation Office Competition [disaster control planning]: the winning entry and two 'Highly Commended' entries.* London: NPO, 1989.

Revill, Don (ed.). *Working papers on disaster management.* SCONUL, 1995. (SCONUL Working Papers.)

Zurich Municipal Loss Control Services. *Local authority library contingency plan; Local authority library and museum contingency plan.* Zurich Municipal: Farnborough, 1996. (With computer disk and hard copy. Both plans in wordprocessor format for customisation by individual libraries. Available in three formats: Ami Pro 3.1, MS Word for Windows 6.0 and Wordperfect 5.x Copies available from Zurich Municipal Loss Control Services.)

NOTES